"This book is full of recipes that are a perfect answer to that 'what's for dinner?' question we all get! Valerie has provided so many easy and delicious mealtime solutions."

—LEIGH ANNE WILKES, author of *Holiday Slow Cooker* and creator of
Your Homebased Mom

"This will hands-down be your go-to slow cooker cookbook for scrumptious dinners the whole family will enjoy . . . The recipes are easy to follow, simple to prepare and flavorful."

—AMY BRINKLEY, creator of The Blond Cook

"Valerie is a master at making recipes approachable and inviting. Her use of easy-to-find ingredients and easy-to-understand instructions are just a few of the hallmarks of this foolproof cookbook."

—BRANDIE SKIBINSKI, creator of The Country Cook

"Wonderful recipes for slow cooker lovers! These are perfect for taking the hassle out of meal planning."

—SARAH OLSON, creator of The Magical Slow Cooker

"This book is an absolute lifesaver for your busy family. You will not believe how much time you will save and how much better your family will be eating!"

—KAREN GIFFORD, creator of The Food Charlatan

The

FOOLPROOF
FAMILY
SLOW COOKER

AND OTHER ONE-POT SOLUTIONS

EASY, DELICIOUS RECIPES
THAT COME OUT PERFECT EVERY TIME

VALERIE BRUNMEIER
FOUNDER OF VALERIE'S KITCHEN

PAGE STREET
PUBLISHING CO.

PAGE STREET
PUBLISHING CO.

First published in 2019 by
Page Street Publishing Co.
27 Congress Street, Suite 105
Salem, MA 01970
www.pagestreetpublishing.com

Distributed by Macmillan, sales in Canada by The Canadian Manda Group.

23   22   21   20   19   1   2   3   4   5

ISBN-13: 978-1-62414-758-6
ISBN-10: 1-62414-758-5

Library of Congress Control Number: 2018964657

Cover and book design by Meg Baskis for Page Street Publishing Co.
Photography by Valerie Brunmeier and Jake Brunmeier
Cover image © Valerie Brunmeier
Family photo on dedication page by Lynna Nguyen Photography
Headshot on author page by Kita Roberts Photography

Printed and bound in China

To **MY HUSBAND, PAUL—**

YOU MADE ME BELIEVE ANYTHING WAS POSSIBLE AND YOU WERE RIGHT.
NO GUTS, NO GLORY, HONEY. I CAN'T WAIT TO SEE WHERE WE GO NEXT.

To **MY BOYS, RYAN, JAKE, CONNOR AND ADAM—**

SMART, COMPASSIONATE, FUNNY, HELPFUL, INDEPENDENT THINKERS, JUST LIKE YOUR DAD.
YOU ARE THE THING THAT I WANTED TO DO MOST IN THIS LIFE . . . THE REST IS GRAVY.

CONTENTS

INTRODUCTION

Between work, school, shuttling your kids to all their activities and trying to find time for yourself every now and then, getting a wholesome family meal on the table can seem like an impossible task. This cookbook was created with your busy life in mind! Its collection of practical, approachable recipes will help you cook satisfying, mouthwatering meals for your family that require little effort and minimal cleanup without skimping on flavor or quality. You'll find over fifty slow-cooker recipes ⬤ with some fun flavor twists, and for those days when even a small amount of morning prep is impossible, there are over twenty one-pot solutions 🍳 that can be prepared quickly and easily at the end of a hectic day. Some recipes even have options for both!

As the mom of four grown sons, I understand the struggle of feeding a busy family. I spent years scurrying to prepare late-night dinners after baseball games that went far too long (in this mom's opinion) and weekend water polo tournaments that kept me out of the house for a good part of the day. These recipes reflect the tastes of my now-grown boys and are perfect for everything from game-day parties to backyard barbecues and holiday gatherings.

My cooking philosophy is simple and practical. Homemade is best, but I firmly defend making use of good-quality store-bought items, like barbecue and marinara sauces, to speed along an otherwise impossible dinner. We have limited time in our busy lives, and shortcuts are a necessary and completely acceptable part of home cooking in my book.

I'm also big on method. For example, I use a lot of dried herbs and spices because they hold up better than fresh herbs, which break down and lose their intensity if cooked too long. Fresh is not always best when it comes to slow cooking. That said, I love to brighten up a recipe with fresh herbs, but I wait until close to the end of the cooking time to get the most out of them. It's the same with canned beans—they become mushy and take on an unappealing texture if cooked for an extended amount of time in the slow cooker, so I recommend adding them about thirty to sixty minutes before the end. Little tips and tricks like these that are often left out of recipes make all the difference. Their absence is why recipes passed down from your aunt or your grandmother don't turn out quite the same when you make them yourself. I've included as many tips and tricks as possible to help you yield the best result.

You may notice I incorporate a lot of fresh vegetables in my recipes. This is something I've always done, and now I have a group of vegetable-loving adults as a result. I've found that if you prepare them the right way, even the pickiest little eater will gobble them up! These recipes are approachable enough for your biggest vegetable skeptic and will appeal to family members of all ages. And with options for both lighter, lower calorie dishes and heartier, more indulgent fare, they'll appeal to every appetite as well.

It's my hope that many of the dishes in this collection will become family favorites, and that you'll learn new techniques and methods along the way. Mealtimes bring the family together, and these recipes will help you create delicious, stress-free fare to make those moments even more enjoyable.

Valerie Brunmeier

POULTRY

The recipes in this chapter span a variety of cuisines and flavors that reflect my family's tastes. They are tailored to appeal to every age group so you can introduce your little ones to new and interesting flavors and encourage them to become more adventurous eaters. Preparing meals for your family is so much more fun and gives you a world of options when you are feeding a group who loves a variety of cuisines.

If you're looking to satisfy a craving for Mexican food, the Stacked Chicken Enchilada Casserole (page 15) will hit the spot. Or make the Green-Chile Chicken Tacos with Corn Salsa (page 24) and let your slow cooker do all the work of creating tender, shreddable chicken. For a quick and easy one-pot solution, look to the Loaded Chicken and Veggie Fajitas (page 33).

The Italian-inspired Chicken Parmesan Meatball Subs (page 29) are extremely family friendly and include a make-ahead option that allows you to get most of the prep out of the way in advance. And the ability to easily control the spice level in the Chicken Tikka Masala with Cauliflower and Red Bell Pepper (page 27) will have you eager to make this classic and comforting Indian dish at home.

Familiar American flavors make an appearance in Fall-off-the-Bone Homestyle Chicken and Gravy (page 13) and the super kid-friendly, one-pot Creamy Chicken and Rice with Peas and Carrots (page 37). And if you have teenagers in your house, I can pretty much guarantee they will devour the Barbecue Chicken Sheet-Pan Quesadillas (page 23).

FALL-OFF-THE-BONE HOMESTYLE CHICKEN AND GRAVY

Most home cooks have a bottle of poultry seasoning in their pantry but use it only once a year on Thanksgiving. This is such a shame because it is an excellent way to instantly create a cozy, home-style flavor in poultry dishes all through the year. In this recipe, I combine it with softened butter and a few other simple seasonings to create a butter rub that adds great flavor to both the chicken and easy gravy. Serve it with mashed or roasted potatoes and the vegetable of your choice. My guys absolutely love this comforting meal!

The key to this recipe is elevating the chicken above the broth as it cooks, which essentially lets the slow cooker steam it to tender perfection.

SERVES 4

HERB AND LEMON BUTTER RUB

¼ cup (56 g) butter, softened

2 tsp (10 g) salt

1 tsp poultry seasoning

1 tsp paprika

½ tsp freshly ground black pepper

½ tsp granulated garlic or garlic powder

½ tsp onion powder

1 lemon, zested

1 large white or yellow onion

1 (5–6 lb [2.3–2.7 kg]) whole chicken

To prepare the rub, combine the butter, salt, poultry seasoning, paprika, black pepper, granulated garlic and onion powder in a small bowl. Add the zest of the lemon and mix until well incorporated. Slice the zested lemon in quarters and set it aside for later.

Slice the onion into three thick slices and remove the outer skin. Place the onion slices on the bottom of your slow cooker. Roll up sheets of foil into balls and place them between the onion slices to fill in any spaces as needed.

Remove the chicken from its packaging and place it on a sheet of foil. Use your hands to thoroughly coat the chicken with the butter rub. Gently lift the skin from both sides of the breast portion and spread some of the butter rub underneath. Place the lemon quarters inside the cavity of the chicken, discarding any that don't fit. Place the chicken, breast side down, on top of the onion slices and foil balls. Cover and cook for 5 to 7 hours on low or 3 to 4 hours on high until the internal temperature reaches 160°F (70°C) in a meaty part of the leg and the juices run clear. The cooking time will vary depending on the weight of your chicken.

If you'd like a browned appearance, you can transfer the chicken to a baking dish and broil it in the oven for several minutes, watching closely, until it's golden brown. Alternatively, transfer the chicken to a cutting board to rest.

Reserve the chicken drippings in the slow cooker for the gravy.

(continued)

FALL-OFF-THE-BONE HOMESTYLE CHICKEN AND GRAVY (CONTINUED)

EASY CHICKEN GRAVY

½ cup (120 ml) reserved chicken drippings

2 tbsp (28 g) butter

3 tbsp (25 g) all-purpose flour

1½ cups (360 ml) low-sodium chicken broth (I like Better Than Bouillon®)

Salt and freshly ground black pepper

To make the gravy, pour the reserved chicken drippings through a fine-mesh sieve to strain out any solids and set it aside.

Add the butter to a medium-heavy saucepan and place it over medium-low heat. Once the butter has melted, sprinkle in the flour. Whisk to make a roux. Whisk and cook the roux until lightly golden brown, about 3 to 5 minutes. Pour in the broth and ½ cup (120 ml) of the strained chicken drippings. Cook and whisk for several minutes until thickened. Taste and season with salt and pepper.

Serve the chicken with mashed or roasted potatoes topped with gravy along with an easy vegetable side dish.

STACKED CHICKEN ENCHILADA CASSEROLE

Enchiladas are one of the most requested meals in our house, and this slow-cooker casserole definitely hits the spot when we're craving Mexican. The filling uses previously cooked chicken, like my All-Purpose Chicken (page 41) or a store-bought rotisserie chicken, and it takes just a couple of minutes to mix together. My favorite semi-homemade enchilada sauce comes together quickly and can be made in advance to save time. For the tortillas, I suggest using 50/50-blend corn and flour tortillas if you can find them. They are great for soft tacos, but they also hold up well in slow-cooker recipes. Most importantly, they taste fabulous.

SERVES 6 TO 8

EASY RED ENCHILADA SAUCE

2 tbsp (30 ml) vegetable oil

3 tbsp (25 g) flour

1 cup (240 ml) low-sodium beef broth

1 (15-oz [425-g]) can red enchilada sauce (use Hatch® brand if you can find it)

1 tsp ground cumin

¼ tsp salt

Freshly ground black pepper, to taste

ENCHILADA FILLING

4 cups (500 g) shredded All-Purpose Chicken (page 41) or store-bought rotisserie chicken

¾ cup (180 g) sour cream

1 cup (120 g) shredded Monterey Jack cheese

1 (4-oz [115-g]) can mild diced green chiles, drained

½ tsp salt

Freshly ground black pepper, to taste

To make the sauce, heat the vegetable oil in a medium saucepan over low heat. Whisk in the flour and cook, whisking constantly, for a minute or 2 until the mixture is just beginning to turn golden brown. Whisk in the broth, enchilada sauce, cumin, salt and pepper. Increase the heat to medium-high and bring the mixture to a boil. Reduce the heat enough to keep the mixture at a low simmer, and whisk it lightly for 2 to 3 minutes until thickened. Remove the pan from the heat. Reserve 1 cup (240 ml) of the sauce.

To make the filling, combine the chicken, sour cream, Monterey Jack cheese and diced green chiles in a large mixing bowl. Season the mixture with salt and black pepper.

Coat the insert of a 6-quart (5.5-L) slow cooker with nonstick cooking spray.

(continued)

STACKED CHICKEN ENCHILADA CASSEROLE (CONTINUED)

FOR THE LAYERS

12 (6" [15-cm]) 50/50-blend corn and flour tortillas (I like the ones from La Tortilla Factory)

6 green onions, thinly sliced

2½ cups (300 g) shredded cheese, divided (I use a combination of sharp cheddar and Monterey Jack)

1 (2.25-oz [65-g]) can sliced black olives, drained

OPTIONAL TOPPINGS

Cilantro, avocado, sour cream, diced tomatoes, hot sauce or salsa

Place two tortillas side by side on the bottom of the slow cooker. Break another tortilla in half and place the halves over the two tortillas to cover the empty spaces. Spread one-third of the chicken filling evenly over the top, and sprinkle it with one-quarter of the green onions, ½ cup (120 g) of shredded cheese and one-third of the sauce remaining in the saucepan (save the reserved 1 cup [240 ml] for later). Repeat to make two more layers in the same order. Finish by topping the enchilada stack with the three remaining tortillas. Pour the reserved 1 cup (240 ml) of enchilada sauce over the top and smooth it out with the back of a spoon to cover the tortillas. Sprinkle with the remaining cheese.

Cover and cook on low for 3 to 4 hours. Turn the slow cooker off, remove the cover and sprinkle on the remaining green onions and olives. Let the casserole rest for 15 to 20 minutes before serving.

Scoop out individual servings with a spoon and garnish them with your toppings of choice. I like to serve this with a simple salad and some Mexican rice.

TIP: If you can't find the 50/50-blend tortillas, you can substitute flour tortillas, but watch closely as the cooking time may need to be reduced slightly.

HAWAIIAN BARBECUE CHICKEN SANDWICHES

This flavorful shredded chicken can be used in a variety of ways, but we love it piled on toasted sesame Hawaiian buns that are slathered with a simple pineapple mayonnaise and melted provolone cheese. Refrigerate the leftovers to serve over rice with steamed or roasted vegetables for an easy second meal later in the week. It's also delicious rolled up in tortillas or wraps with shredded cheese and cilantro.

SERVES 8

1 cup (240 ml) barbecue sauce (I like Kinder's Mild BBQ Sauce)

½ cup + 1 tbsp (135 ml) pineapple juice, divided

¼ cup (60 ml) ketchup

¼ cup (60 ml) low-sodium soy sauce

1 tbsp (9 g) brown sugar

1 tsp toasted sesame oil

1 tsp minced garlic

½ tsp ground ginger

2 lbs (910 g) boneless, skinless chicken breasts

½ cup (75 g) diced red onion

¾ cup (165 g) mayonnaise

1 (8-count) package Hawaiian hamburger buns

8 slices provolone cheese

2 tbsp (28 g) butter, melted

2 tbsp (30 g) sesame seeds, or as needed

Coat the insert of a 5 to 6 quart (4.7 to 5.5 L) slow cooker with nonstick cooking spray.

Whisk together the barbecue sauce, ½ cup (120 ml) of pineapple juice, ketchup, soy sauce, brown sugar, sesame oil, minced garlic and ground ginger, and pour half of the sauce mixture into the slow cooker.

Add the chicken to the slow cooker, pour the remaining sauce over the top and sprinkle it with the red onion. Cover and cook for 5 to 6 hours on low, until the chicken is tender and easy to shred. Turn the slow cooker off and use two forks to shred the chicken into the sauce. Let the chicken rest while you prepare the hamburger buns.

Preheat your oven to 400°F (200°C) and coat a large rimmed baking sheet with nonstick cooking spray. Combine the mayonnaise with the reserved 1 tablespoon (15 ml) of pineapple juice in a small bowl and set it aside.

Separate the hamburger buns and place them on the prepared baking sheet, open side up. Bake for several minutes, until lightly toasted. Remove the baking sheet from the oven and spread the bottom halves of the buns with the pineapple mayonnaise. Use tongs to pile some of the shredded chicken on each bottom half, then add a slice of provolone cheese. Cover with the tops, brush them with the melted butter and sprinkle them with the sesame seeds.

Bake for 5 minutes, until the cheese is melted and the tops of the buns are lightly toasted.

TIP: Make the prep even easier by preparing the chicken a day in advance and storing it in an airtight container in the refrigerator overnight. Warm the chicken briefly in the microwave to take the chill off, then assemble and bake the sandwiches as directed.

BRAISED CHICKEN THIGHS WITH SPRING VEGETABLES

Chicken thighs cook up so wonderfully in a short period of time that they are the perfect choice for quick dishes like this one. With a 25-minute simmer in a wine-infused broth, they will be so tender that you'll be able to leave the steak knives in the drawer. They are also such a great value that I try to use them as often as I can. Remove the skin before braising so that the resulting cooking liquids can be spooned over the tender chicken and vegetables when serving. This is a comforting, simple dish.

SERVES 4 TO 6

6–8 bone-in chicken thighs

Salt and freshly ground black pepper, to taste

2 tbsp (28 g) butter

⅓ cup (50 g) diced shallots

1 tsp minced garlic

4 carrots, sliced into 1" (3-cm) pieces

2 celery ribs, chopped

1 cup (240 ml) dry white wine, like sauvignon blanc or pinot grigio

1–2 cups (240–480 ml) low-sodium chicken broth (I like Better Than Bouillon), as needed

1 lemon

1 tbsp (3 g) fresh thyme leaves

1 tbsp (3 g) chopped fresh rosemary

1 bunch of asparagus, trimmed

Remove and discard the skin from the bone-in chicken thighs. Use a sharp knife to trim any large deposits of fat that are left around the edges, and season with salt and pepper.

Melt the butter in a large, deep sauté pan or Dutch oven over medium-high heat. Add the chicken to the pot and brown it for about 4 to 5 minutes per side. Transfer the chicken to a plate and set it aside. Do this in batches, if necessary, to avoid overcrowding the pan.

Reduce the heat to medium, add the shallots, garlic, carrots and celery and sauté for 5 minutes. Add the wine, stirring to scrape up any browned bits from the bottom of the pan, and increase the heat to bring the mixture to a low boil. Return the chicken to the pan, placing it on top of the vegetables. Add enough broth to submerge the chicken about halfway (the chicken should not be totally covered by broth) and bring the liquid to a simmer. Squeeze the juice from the lemon over the top and sprinkle the chicken with the thyme and rosemary. Cover the pot and let it simmer on medium-low for 20 minutes.

Remove the lid and scatter the asparagus over the top. Cover and continue to cook for an additional 5 to 7 minutes, until the chicken is cooked through and the asparagus is fork-tender. Season with additional salt and pepper.

BARBECUE CHICKEN SHEET-PAN QUESADILLAS

My boys love quesadillas, but with the standard skillet method there is always that long wait while you stand at the stove cooking them in batches. This sheet-pan method allows you to cook four quesadillas all at once with just one bowl to wash after dinner. Double the recipe and use two sheet pans for a bigger group. Making use of cooked, shredded chicken allows you to create this delicious meal in 30 minutes or less.

SERVES 4

½ cup (120 ml) barbecue sauce (I like Kinder's Mild BBQ Sauce)

¼ cup (60 ml) red salsa (your favorite brand)

1 (4-oz [115-g]) can diced green chiles, drained

2 tbsp (8 g) diced red onion

2 cups (250 g) shredded All-Purpose Chicken (page 41) or store-bought rotisserie chicken

4 (8" [20-cm]) flour tortillas

¾ cup (90 g) shredded sharp cheddar cheese, divided

¾ cup (90 g) shredded Monterey Jack cheese, divided

⅓ cup (15 g) roughly chopped cilantro leaves, divided, plus more for garnish

2 tbsp (30 ml) vegetable oil, or as needed

OPTIONAL TOPPINGS

Sour cream and additional salsa

Preheat the oven to 425°F (220°C). Line a 12 × 17-inch (30 × 45-cm) rimmed baking sheet with parchment paper or foil and spray it with nonstick cooking spray to keep the baking sheet clean and prevent any filling that spills out from burning.

Combine the barbecue sauce, salsa, green chiles and red onion in a medium mixing bowl. Add the shredded chicken and toss the mixture to combine it well.

Spread one-quarter of the filling mixture on one half of a flour tortilla. Sprinkle it with one-quarter of the cheddar and Monterey Jack cheeses and one-quarter of the cilantro. Fold the tortilla in half. Repeat with the three remaining tortillas. Brush the tops of the quesadillas with vegetable oil.

Cover the quesadillas with a second sheet of parchment paper or foil, and place a second rimmed baking sheet over the top to weigh them down and help hold their shape while they bake. Bake for 10 minutes. Remove the pans from the oven and take off the top baking sheet and parchment paper. Return the uncovered baking sheet to the oven for an additional 10 to 12 minutes, until the cheese has melted and the tops of quesadillas are crisped and golden brown. Remove the baking sheet from the oven and allow the quesadillas to rest for about 3 minutes. Don't be concerned if some of the filling has spilled out. The quesadillas will set up and slice well after resting.

Transfer the quesadillas to a cutting board and use a sharp knife to cut each quesadilla in half. Garnish with cilantro, and serve them with sour cream and salsa for dipping.

GREEN-CHILE CHICKEN TACOS WITH CORN SALSA

This is a recipe to be excited about if you have fans of Mexican food in your house. There is very little prep, but you would never know it by the incredible results. It's literally one of those recipes that lets you just toss everything in the slow cooker and walk away. When you come back, you will have perfectly tender chicken that you can shred right into the slow-cooked green-chile sauce. After you get the chicken cooking in the morning, you can whip up the Easy Corn Salsa and chill it until you are ready to serve dinner, or just throw it together right before you are ready to serve. This versatile shredded chicken is fantastic in a variety of Mexican dishes.

SERVES 8

TACOS

2¼–2½ lbs (1.1–1.2 kg) boneless, skinless chicken breast

1½ tsp (5 g) cumin

½ tsp granulated garlic or garlic powder

½ tsp salt

Freshly ground black pepper

¾ cup (95 g) diced onion

1 (15-oz [425-g]) can green enchilada sauce (I like Hatch Green Chile Enchilada Sauce)

1 (4-oz [115-g]) can diced green chiles, drained

½ cup (20 g) chopped cilantro

6" (15-cm) tortillas, as needed (you can use flour, corn or 50/50-blend tortillas)

EASY CORN SALSA

2 cups (290 g) frozen corn, completely thawed and drained

¼ cup (35 g) diced red onion

1 jalapeño, seeded and diced

¼ cup (10 g) chopped cilantro

½ lime, juiced

¼ tsp salt, or to taste

OPTIONAL TOPPINGS

Crumbled cotija cheese, diced tomatoes, avocado, sour cream

Lay the chicken along the bottom of a 6-quart (5.5-L) slow cooker. Sprinkle it with the cumin, granulated garlic, salt and pepper. Scatter the onion over the top, then cover it with the enchilada sauce and chiles.

Cover and cook for 7 to 8 hours on low or 5 to 6 hours on high, until the chicken is very tender and easy to shred. Turn off and unplug the slow cooker and use two forks to shred the chicken into the sauce. Stir in the cilantro.

To prepare the corn salsa, combine the corn, red onion, jalapeño, cilantro, lime juice and salt in a medium mixing bowl. The salsa can be prepared up to 8 hours in advance and stored in the refrigerator in an airtight container.

To toast the tortillas, place a dry skillet over medium heat and add a tortilla. Let it cook for a couple of minutes per side, until toasted to your desired level. Repeat with the remaining tortillas.

Serve the chicken on the toasted tortillas with corn salsa and the toppings of your choice.

CHICKEN TIKKA MASALA WITH CAULIFLOWER AND RED BELL PEPPER

If you haven't had the pleasure of trying tikka masala, I'm betting it will be love at first bite. It's very appropriately described as Indian comfort food and includes tender chunks of chicken that are simmered in a creamy tomato-based sauce infused with fragrant and highly flavorful Indian spices, including curry and garam masala.

If you order tikka masala at a restaurant, the heat level can range from mild to pretty darn spicy, but when you make it at home, you can easily adjust the spice level to your liking. Use fewer red pepper flakes for a mildly spicy dish, or add more to really rev it up. Your house will smell amazing as this aromatic mix simmers away throughout the day. This recipe appears on my menu regularly.

SERVES 6

2 tbsp (30 ml) olive oil

1 cup (150 g) chopped white or yellow onion

2 tsp (10 g) peeled and finely grated ginger root

2 tsp (6 g) minced garlic

1 (14.5-oz [410-g]) can fire-roasted diced tomatoes, undrained

1 (14.5-oz [410-g]) can tomato sauce

4 tsp (12 g) garam masala

2 tsp (6 g) curry powder

2 tsp (6 g) cumin

1 tsp paprika

1 tsp salt

½ tsp–1 tsp red pepper flakes, to taste

2–2½ lbs (0.9–1.2 kg) boneless, skinless chicken breasts or thighs (or a combination)

1 head cauliflower, cut into small florets

1 large red bell pepper, sliced into 2" (5-cm) julienne strips

SLOW-COOKER METHOD
Add the olive oil to a large skillet and place it over medium-high heat. Add the onion, ginger root and garlic to the pan and cook for several minutes, until softened, stirring occasionally. Stir in the tomatoes and tomato sauce. Add the garam masala, curry powder, cumin, paprika, salt and red pepper flakes. Bring the mixture to a boil, then reduce the heat to low and allow it to simmer while you prepare the chicken.

Cut the chicken into bite-size chunks and place them in a 6-quart (5.5-L) slow cooker. Pour the mixture from the skillet over the chicken and stir it well to coat the chicken with the sauce. Scatter the cauliflower over the top. Do not stir. Cover and cook for 5 to 6 hours on low or 3 hours on high, until the chicken is tender.

Add the bell pepper to the slow cooker and stir it and the cauliflower into the sauce. Cover and cook for an additional 30 to 40 minutes, until the vegetables are fork-tender.

(continued)

1 (13.5-oz [380-g]) can coconut milk, divided

2 tbsp (20 g) cornstarch

¼ cup (10 g) chopped fresh cilantro, for garnish

3 cups (680 g) cooked long-grain or jasmine rice, for serving

Plain Greek yogurt, for topping, optional

Shake the can of coconut milk well and measure out ¼ cup (60 ml). Add the cornstarch to the measuring cup with the coconut milk and stir it until it is well combined and the cornstarch has dissolved. Add the remaining coconut milk to the slow cooker, stirring it into the chicken and sauce. Add the cornstarch slurry and stir again until well combined. Cover and continue to cook for an additional 5 to 10 minutes, until the sauce is slightly thickened and heated through.

Garnish with cilantro and serve over rice. Top each serving with a dollop of Greek yogurt, if desired.

ONE-POT METHOD
Cut the chicken into bite-size chunks and set aside.

Add the olive oil to a Dutch oven and place it over medium-high heat. Add the chicken, onion, ginger root and garlic to the pan and cook for 4 or 5 minutes, until the chicken is mostly cooked through and the onion has softened, stirring occasionally. Add the garam masala, curry powder, cumin, paprika, salt and red pepper flakes. Cook for 2 to 3 minutes while stirring to coat the chicken with the spices. Stir in the tomatoes, tomato sauce, cauliflower and bell pepper.

Shake the can of coconut milk well and measure out ¼ cup (60 ml). Add the cornstarch to the measuring cup with the coconut milk and stir it until it is well combined and the cornstarch has dissolved. Add the remaining coconut milk to the Dutch oven. Add the cornstarch slurry and stir again until well combined. Bring the mixture to a boil, then reduce the heat to medium-low and simmer, covered, for 30 to 40 minutes, until the chicken and cauliflower are tender and the sauce has thickened.

Garnish with cilantro and serve over rice. Top each serving with a dollop of Greek yogurt, if desired.

> TIP: After peeling the ginger root, I use my microplane to finely grate it, resulting in a consistency that practically melts into sauces and marinades. If you have leftover ginger root, place it in a freezer-safe plastic storage bag and pop it in the freezer. It will stay fresh longer and grate much easier frozen.

CHICKEN PARMESAN MEATBALL SUBS

Using lean ground chicken eliminates the need for any advance browning or baking. You can put these tasty meatballs straight into your slow cooker, and they will cook up perfectly tender in the hot sauce, leaving very little grease behind. My boys love them piled on hoagie rolls with melted provolone cheese, but they are also delicious with the cooked pasta of your choice, topped with plenty of shredded Parmesan.

The meatballs will seem very soft and a bit sticky after they are formed but will firm up nicely and hold their shape after they are chilled. I like to make them a day in advance and refrigerate them overnight for super quick prep the next morning.

SERVES 6

MEATBALLS

2 large eggs

2 lbs (910 g) ground chicken

1 cup (40 g) Italian-style panko bread crumbs

½ cup (90 g) finely grated Parmesan cheese

⅓ cup (66 g) grated onion

1 tsp minced garlic

2 tsp (2 g) dried parsley

2 tsp (2 g) dried basil

1 tsp salt

½ tsp freshly ground black pepper

To make the meatballs, crack the eggs into a large mixing bowl and whisk them lightly. Add the chicken, bread crumbs, Parmesan, onion, garlic, parsley, basil, salt and pepper, and using your hands, mix and knead the mixture to combine it well.

Form the mixture into 28 meatballs about 1½ inches (4 cm) in diameter. The mixture will be a bit sticky, so wet your hands as needed to make rolling the meatballs easier. Place the meatballs on a foil-lined baking sheet, and cover them with another sheet of foil. Refrigerate for at least 1 hour or more. The meatballs can be prepared in advance and refrigerated for up to 24 hours.

(continued)

SAUCE

1 (28-oz [800-g]) can Italian-style crushed tomatoes

1 (24–26-oz [680–740-g]) jar marinara sauce

½ cup (120 ml) water

¼ cup (35 g) finely chopped onion

1 tsp minced garlic

1 tsp Italian seasoning

¼ tsp red pepper flakes, or to taste

Salt and freshly ground black pepper, to taste

½ cup (120 ml) heavy cream

2 tbsp (6 g) chopped fresh basil

SUBS

6 hoagie rolls

6 oz (170 g) mozzarella or provolone cheese, sliced

To make the sauce, add the tomatoes, marinara, water, onion, garlic, Italian seasoning, red pepper flakes, salt and pepper to the slow cooker. Cover and cook for 1 hour on high.

When the sauce is done, place the refrigerated meatballs into the sauce, reshaping them into nice balls as you add them. Spoon the sauce over any exposed meatballs so that they are all immersed in sauce. Cover and cook for 4 to 6 hours on low, until the meatballs are thoroughly cooked. Avoid stirring the meatballs during cooking to help them keep their shape.

Once the meatballs are cooked through, stir in the cream and basil. Cover and continue to cook for 5 minutes.

Preheat your oven to broil, and place the opened (but intact) hoagie rolls on a large rimmed baking sheet. Broil them briefly, until the bread is toasted. Remove the baking sheet from the oven and top the toasted rolls with the meatballs and sliced cheese. Return the baking sheet to the oven, and broil for 1 to 2 minutes, watching closely, until the cheese has melted.

TIP: Use a cheese grater to grate the onion before adding it to the meatball mixture. Grated onion practically melts into the meatballs as they cook, adding great flavor and ensuring tender, smooth meatballs.

LOADED CHICKEN AND VEGGIE FAJITAS

A local Mexican restaurant provided the inspiration for this simple dish. They serve their fajitas with the typical combination of bell peppers and onions, but also include strips of zucchini. Such a simple thing, but truly a revelation. Zucchini is so meaty and wonderful wrapped in a tortilla along with the traditional fajita veggies and deliciously seasoned chicken. For even more vibrant color and a sweet bite, I also add sweet corn to the mix. While fresh corn on the cob is always wonderful, frozen corn will absolutely do the trick, and you don't even need to thaw it out before you toss it in the skillet. This meal comes together quickly, but make sure you set aside time for the chicken to marinate for at least two hours or overnight.

SERVES 6

2 lbs (910 g) boneless, skinless chicken breast

7 tbsp (105 ml) olive oil, divided

5 tbsp (45 g) Smoky Fajita Seasoning Mix (page 185), divided

1 lime, halved

2 bell peppers of assorted colors, cored, seeded and sliced into thin strips

1 yellow onion, peeled, halved and sliced into thin strips

1 zucchini, halved and cut into strips

1 ear of sweet corn (husked and kernels sliced from the cob) or ½ cup (70 g) frozen corn kernels

1 tsp minced garlic

Fajita-size (6" [15-cm]) flour tortillas, as needed

OPTIONAL TOPPINGS

Cilantro, avocado, crumbled cotija cheese, sour cream, salsa or hot sauce

Cut each chicken breast in half and place it in a zippered gallon-size (3.8-L) plastic storage bag or other airtight container. Combine 4 tablespoons (60 ml) of olive oil, 4 tablespoons (36 g) of Smoky Fajita Seasoning Mix and the juice from one lime half in a small bowl to make a thick rub. Pour the mixture over the chicken in the bag. Move the chicken around in the bag until it is completely coated, seal the bag and transfer it to the refrigerator to marinate for at least 2 hours and up to 8 hours.

Add 2 tablespoons (30 ml) of olive oil to a 12-inch (30-cm) cast-iron or other heavy skillet and place it over medium heat. Add the chicken and cook for about 4 minutes per side, until cooked through. Transfer the cooked chicken to a cutting board and tent it loosely with aluminum foil while you cook the veggies.

Add an additional 1 tablespoon (15 ml) of olive oil to the skillet and place it over medium heat. Add the peppers and onion and cook, stirring, for 3 to 4 minutes, until crisp-tender. Add the zucchini strips, corn and garlic to the skillet. Sprinkle them with the remaining 1 tablespoon (9 g) of Smoky Fajita Seasoning Mix and cook, stirring, for another 3 or 4 minutes until the zucchini is fork-tender. Remove the pan from the heat.

Slice the chicken into thin strips and squeeze the juice from the remaining lime half over the top.

To toast the tortillas, place a dry skillet over medium heat and add a tortilla. Let it cook for a couple of minutes per side, until toasted to your desired level. Repeat with the remaining tortillas.

Serve the chicken and veggies on the toasted flour tortillas, with the optional toppings if you like.

BARBECUE CHICKEN DRUMSTICKS

After a turn in the slow cooker, these incredibly tender chicken drumsticks are finished off in the oven, where a coating of my Best-Ever Barbecue Seasoning Mix and bottled barbecue sauce caramelize together to create a sticky, deliciously seasoned exterior. Drumsticks are a fantastic value which makes this recipe an awesome choice for a big gathering, and since no grill is required, they can be on the menu any time of year. Be sure to have plenty of napkins on hand!

SERVES 8

4 lbs (1.8 kg) chicken drumsticks, skin on

1 batch of Best-Ever Barbecue Seasoning Mix (page 185)

¾ cup (180 ml) bottled barbecue sauce (I like Kinder's Mild BBQ Sauce)

Coat the insert of a 6-quart (5.5-L) slow cooker with nonstick cooking spray. Place the chicken in a large mixing bowl and toss with the Best-Ever Barbecue Seasoning Mix. Transfer the seasoned chicken to the slow cooker. Cover and cook for 4 to 5 hours on low, until the chicken is very tender and a meat thermometer registers 165°F (70°C) when inserted into the meaty part of the drumstick.

Place your oven rack about 7 inches (18 cm) from the heating element, and set your oven to broil. Line a large rimmed baking sheet with aluminum foil and coat the foil with nonstick cooking spray. Transfer the chicken to the baking sheet and brush the top side liberally with barbecue sauce. Broil the drumsticks for 4 to 5 minutes, watching closely to be sure they don't burn. Remove the baking sheet from the oven, flip the drumsticks and brush the other side with additional barbecue sauce. Return the baking sheet to the oven for an additional 4 to 5 minutes, until the sauce is caramelized. Remove the baking sheet from the oven, brush the drumsticks lightly with the remaining barbecue sauce and serve.

CREAMY CHICKEN AND RICE WITH PEAS AND CARROTS

A comforting combination of familiar flavors, this dish cooks up quickly in one pan. I can't have enough recipes like this at my disposal for busy times, and this one is particularly family friendly with chicken, creamy, cheesy rice and peas and carrots. I'm always happy to reheat leftovers of this tasty one-pot meal for lunch the following day.

SERVES 4 TO 6

2 tbsp (28 g) butter

1 lb (450 g) boneless, skinless chicken breasts, cut into bite-size pieces

1 tsp dried thyme

1 tsp salt, divided

¼ tsp freshly ground black pepper, or to taste

1 cup (125 g) peeled and chopped carrots (about 2 large carrots)

1 cup (100 g) chopped celery (about 2 ribs)

1 cup (150 g) diced yellow onion

1 tsp minced garlic

1½ cups (165 g) uncooked long-grain white rice

2 cups (480 ml) low-sodium chicken broth (I like Better Than Bouillon)

1½ cups (360 ml) whole milk

1 cup (145 g) frozen baby peas

2 tbsp (6 g) chopped fresh Italian parsley

½ cup (45 g) grated Parmesan cheese

1½ cups (180 g) shredded sharp cheddar cheese, divided

Add the butter to a deep 14-inch (35-cm) skillet or sauté pan with a lid, and place the pan over medium-high heat. When the butter has melted, add the chicken, thyme, ½ teaspoon of salt and the black pepper. Cook for 4 to 5 minutes, stirring occasionally, until golden brown and cooked through.

Add the carrots, celery, onion and garlic, and cook for about 2 minutes, stirring occasionally. Add the rice, broth and milk. Bring the liquid to a boil. Reduce the heat so that the liquid is at a low simmer. Cover the skillet and cook for 15 to 20 minutes, until the rice is tender.

Remove the skillet from the heat and stir in the baby peas, parsley, Parmesan and 1 cup (120 g) of the cheddar cheese. Sprinkle the remaining ½ cup (60 g) of cheddar over the top and cover the skillet again. Allow it to rest, covered, for 5 minutes to melt the cheddar topping.

BARBECUE TURKEY JOES

There's nothing boring about this flavorful take on sloppy joes. Barbecue sauce, pickled jalapeños and a wonderful blend of seasonings add a zingy, smoky kick. Best yet, you'll have this dinner on the table in less than 30 minutes. I like to top ours with shredded pepper Jack cheese, but they are also delicious all on their own. Mild pickled jalapeños add tangy flavor but not much heat to this recipe. Go with the hot variety if your gang likes things spicy. I've been known to spoon leftovers over a baked potato for an easy second meal.

SERVES 6

1 tbsp (15 ml) olive oil

2 lbs (910 g) lean ground turkey

1 cup (150 g) diced white onion

1 small green bell pepper, seeded and diced

1 (14.5-oz [410-g]) can tomato sauce

½ cup (120 ml) ketchup

½ cup (120 ml) barbecue sauce (I like Kinder's Mild BBQ Sauce)

¼ cup (40 g) diced pickled jalapeños, mild or hot

1 tbsp (15 ml) Worcestershire sauce

1 tbsp (9 g) Best-Ever Barbecue Seasoning Mix (page 185)

2 tsp (10 g) prepared yellow mustard

1 tsp cumin

8 onion rolls or hamburger buns, toasted

2 cups (240 g) shredded pepper Jack cheese, optional

Add the olive oil to a deep 14-inch (35-cm) skillet or sauté pan, and place it over medium heat. Add the turkey, onion and bell pepper, and cook, stirring to break up the meat, until no pink remains, 4 to 5 minutes. Drain off as much grease from the skillet as possible and return it to the heat.

Add the tomato sauce, ketchup, barbecue sauce, pickled jalapeños, Worcestershire sauce, Best-Ever Barbecue Seasoning Mix, mustard and cumin. Stir to combine the mixture well. Reduce the heat to low and simmer, uncovered, for 10 minutes, stirring occasionally.

Pile the mixture on the buns, top with the pepper Jack cheese and serve immediately. If you'd like to melt the cheese, set your oven to broil, assemble the sandwiches on a baking sheet—leaving off the tops—and place the baking sheet in the oven for just 1 to 2 minutes.

ALL-PURPOSE CHICKEN

One of the best ways to ensure quick and easy dinners through the week is to cook up a batch of this All-Purpose Chicken on the weekend. While a store-bought rotisserie chicken will do the trick for some recipes, you can easily make your own with the help of your slow cooker. I go very light and simple on the seasoning so that this versatile chicken can be used in a variety of ways.

YIELDS 2 POUNDS (910 G)

2 lbs (910 g) boneless, skinless chicken breast

1 cup (240 ml) low-sodium chicken broth (I like Better Than Bouillon)

3–4 cloves garlic, peeled and halved

½ tsp all-purpose seasoning (I like Lawry's® Seasoned Salt)

Place the chicken in a 4-quart (3.8-L) or larger slow cooker, add the broth, scatter the garlic around the chicken and sprinkle the chicken with the all-purpose seasoning. Cover the slow cooker and cook for 4 to 5 hours on low or for 2 to 3 hours on high, until the chicken is fork-tender and registers an internal temperature of at least 165°F (70°C).

Transfer the cooked chicken to a cutting board and use two forks to shred it, or use a sharp knife to chop it into bite-size pieces, as desired. Reserve the cooking juices. Discard the garlic.

To store the cooked and cooled chicken, transfer it to a zippered gallon-size (3.8-L) plastic storage bag, or other airtight container, along with a small amount of the cooking juices to help keep the chicken moist. It will keep in the refrigerator for up to 3 days or in the freezer for up to 3 months.

BEEF AND PORK

Some of the very first recipes that sold me on slow cooking involved tough cuts of beef, like chuck roast, that evolved into meltingly tender, shreddable meat at the end of the hands-off cooking process. Since then, I've experimented with a large variety of different cuts, and I've incorporated what I've learned into the recipes in this chapter. I'm aiming to show you how your slow cooker can do so much more than pot roast. It makes easy work of creating Tender Slow-Cooked Pork Chops with Creamy Mushroom Gravy (page 46) and Cajun Barbecue Ribs (page 53). It will turn a lean cut of pork into flavorful Pulled Pork with Root Beer Barbecue Sauce (page 62) that is delicious piled on toasted hamburger buns. For a super easy meal, make tacos or burrito bowls with tender Smoky Chipotle Shredded Beef (page 61) and a variety of toppings.

If meatloaf is as popular in your house as it is in ours, your family is going to love the two meatloaf recipes in this chapter. I think you will find the special slow-cooker technique I've included will make all the difference.

For those times when you need to pull off a quick, no-fuss dinner (every night?), I've also included three one-pot choices that are seriously ready in nothing flat and leave you with just one pan to clean. My guys love the 20-Minute Egg Roll Lettuce Wraps (page 50), and you can set your timer if you don't believe me—they honestly take just twenty minutes to prepare from start to finish. This lighter choice is a great way to add some balance to your weekly menu and give yourself a break.

TERIYAKI STEAK TIPS WITH PEPPERS AND MUSHROOMS

Cubes of sirloin steak are slow cooked with bell pepper, onion and mushrooms in a made-from-scratch teriyaki sauce until perfectly tender. Ladle a big scoop over cooked rice to satisfy those take-out cravings.

Top sirloin is under-utilized in my opinion. It is a pretty good value as far as steak goes and priced similarly to flank steak, the cut commonly used for steak teriyaki. In this recipe, it creates dependably tender, meaty and luscious beef tips.

SERVES 6

TERIYAKI SAUCE

⅔ cup (160 ml) light soy sauce

⅔ cup (160 ml) mirin (sweet rice wine)

¼ cup (50 g) sugar

2 tbsp (30 ml) toasted sesame oil

1 tsp peeled and finely grated ginger root

1 tsp minced garlic

⅓ cup (80 ml) water

STEAK TIPS

¼ cup (60 ml) vegetable oil, divided

3 lb (1.3 kg) top sirloin steak, cut into 1–2" (3–5-cm) cubes

Salt and freshly ground black pepper

1 cup (150 g) diced white onion

1 red bell pepper, cut into 1" (3-cm) pieces

1 green bell pepper, cut into 1" (3-cm) pieces

8 oz (225 g) cremini mushrooms, quartered

3 tbsp (45 ml) water

3 tbsp (30 g) cornstarch

3 tbsp (9 g) thinly sliced green onions

2 tsp (10 g) sesame seeds

3 cups (680 g) cooked rice, for serving

For the teriyaki sauce, in a small bowl whisk together the soy sauce, mirin, sugar, sesame oil, ginger, garlic and water. Set it aside.

For the steak tips, heat 2 tablespoons (30 ml) of oil in a 12-inch (30-cm) cast-iron skillet over medium-high heat. When the oil is hot, add half of the beef cubes and season them with the salt and pepper. Allow them to cook undisturbed for a couple of minutes, then stir, cooking just long enough to sear the beef without cooking it through, about 3 or 4 minutes. Use a slotted spoon to transfer the browned beef to the slow cooker. Add the remaining 2 tablespoons (30 ml) of oil to the pan and repeat with the remaining beef cubes.

Add the teriyaki sauce mixture to the slow cooker with the beef. Layer the onion and bell peppers over the top, and without stirring, cover and cook for 6 to 7 hours on low or for 3 to 4 hours on high, until the beef is fork-tender. Add the mushrooms, cover and continue to cook for an additional 20 to 30 minutes on low, just until the mushrooms have softened.

Combine the water and cornstarch in a small bowl and add the mixture to the slow cooker, stirring for several minutes until the sauce has thickened. Sprinkle on the green onions and sesame seeds and serve over the rice.

TENDER SLOW-COOKED PORK CHOPS WITH CREAMY MUSHROOM GRAVY

These tender chops are reminiscent of the pork chops with mushroom gravy that appeared regularly in suburban kitchens everywhere while I was growing up. For an updated take on the classic mushroom gravy, I've added a blend of spices that mimic the dried-onion soup mix commonly used in vintage recipes, minus the extra sodium. The cream of mushroom soup remains because it makes easy work of creating this fabulously creamy, flavorful gravy, and it honestly just wouldn't be the same without it. The slow cooker is an easy way to ensure tender chops, but for me, this recipe is all about the gravy!

SERVES 4 TO 6

PORK CHOPS

4-6 (1" [3-cm]-thick) bone-in pork loin chops

Salt and freshly ground black pepper

2 tbsp (30 ml) olive oil

CREAMY MUSHROOM GRAVY

½ cup (120 ml) dry sherry or dry white wine (like sauvignon blanc or pinot grigio)

1 (10.75-oz [300-g]) can cream of mushroom soup (I like Campbell's®)

3 cups (720 ml) low-sodium beef broth

2 tbsp (18 g) dried minced onion

2 tsp (2 g) dried parsley

½ tsp onion powder

½ tsp garlic powder

½ tsp dried thyme leaves

¼ tsp paprika

¼ tsp freshly ground black pepper

⅓ cup (80 ml) milk

3 tbsp (30 g) cornstarch

Mashed potatoes, for serving

Season both sides of the pork chops with salt and black pepper.

For the gravy, add the sherry, cream of mushroom soup, broth, dried onion, parsley, onion powder, garlic powder, thyme, paprika and black pepper to the slow cooker. Whisk until the mixture is smooth.

Brown the pork chops by placing a 12- to 14-inch (30- to 35-cm) skillet over medium-high heat and adding the olive oil. When the oil is hot, add as many of the pork chops as you can without crowding, and sear them for 2 to 3 minutes per side, until nicely browned. Brown the chops in batches, if necessary, and transfer them to the slow cooker. Push the pork chops down into the cooking liquid, then cover and cook them for 6 to 8 hours on low, until they are fork-tender and have an internal temperature of 160°F (70°C). Transfer the cooked pork chops to a serving platter and cover them with foil to keep warm.

Whisk together the milk and cornstarch, add the mixture to the cooking liquid in the slow cooker and stir until thickened.

Serve the pork chops with mashed potatoes and plenty of the creamy mushroom gravy. A simple vegetable side, such as green beans, will perfectly complement this meal.

SMOKY-SWEET GLAZED MEATLOAF WITH BUTTER-PARSLEY POTATOES

A foil bowl holds this classic meatloaf as it cooks above a bed of butter-parsley potatoes. The slow cooker yields a melt-in-your-mouth result, but with a consistency that holds together and slices beautifully. Serve it with a salad and a batch of Perfectly Tender Skillet Dinner Rolls (page 117).

SERVES 6

MEATLOAF

1 tbsp (14 g) butter

1 cup (150 g) diced white onion

½ cup (20 g) chopped fresh Italian parsley

2 slices of white bread, torn into small pieces

½ cup (120 ml) milk

2 lbs (910 g) lean ground beef

2 large eggs, lightly beaten

⅓ cup (80 ml) ketchup

1 tbsp (15 ml) Worcestershire sauce

1 tsp all-purpose seasoning (I like Lawry's Seasoned Salt)

1 tsp garlic powder

1 tsp dried thyme

½ tsp dried oregano

BUTTER-PARSLEY POTATOES

1½ lbs (675 g) baby Yukon Gold or red potatoes

2 tbsp (28 g) butter, melted

¼ tsp salt

2 tbsp (6 g) chopped fresh Italian parsley

SMOKY-SWEET GLAZE

½ cup (120 ml) ketchup

1 tbsp (15 g) Dijon mustard

1 tbsp (15 g) packed brown sugar

1 tsp smoked paprika

Melt the butter in a 12-inch (30-cm) skillet over medium heat. Add the onion and parsley, and sauté for 3 to 4 minutes, until just tender.

Meanwhile, place the torn bread into a large mixing bowl and add the milk. Stir to coat the bread and allow it to sit for 1 to 2 minutes.

Add the onion and parsley mixture to the bowl with the soaked bread. Add the ground beef, eggs, ketchup, Worcestershire sauce, all-purpose seasoning, garlic powder, thyme and oregano. Mix to incorporate the ingredients, but avoid overworking the meat.

Coat an 18 × 12-inch (45 × 30-cm) sheet of heavy-duty foil with nonstick cooking spray. Turn the meatloaf mixture out onto the foil, and use your hands to form it into an oval loaf, approximately 9 × 6-inches (23 × 15-cm). Fold the edges of the foil up and over to form a bowl around the meatloaf and set it aside.

Add the potatoes, melted butter and salt to the slow cooker. Stir to coat the potatoes with the butter, then spread them out in an even layer along the bottom of the slow cooker. Place the foil bowl containing the meatloaf on top of the potatoes. Cover and cook for 5 to 6 hours on low.

For the glaze, in a small bowl combine the ketchup, mustard, brown sugar and paprika. When the cooking time is up, spread the glaze over the meatloaf, then cover and continue to cook on low for about 30 to 45 minutes until the center of the meatloaf registers 160°F (70°C).

Carefully lift the foil bowl from the slow cooker and drain off the grease. Transfer the meatloaf to a platter and let it rest for 10 minutes before slicing.

Sprinkle the potatoes with parsley and serve them with the meatloaf.

> **TIP:** Use a turkey baster to extract some of the drippings from the foil bowl before lifting it out of the slow cooker. Drain any remaining grease before transferring the meatloaf to the serving platter.

20-MINUTE EGG ROLL LETTUCE WRAPS

This healthier take on egg rolls is packed with cabbage, carrots, bell pepper and lean ground pork or beef that is stir-fried in a slightly sweet and spicy sauce. It will take you about twenty minutes to pull off this dish and way less time for your family to devour it! Fresh mint really brightens up the flavors, but feel free to leave it out if anyone in your family isn't a fan. Served inside tender leaves of butter lettuce, it's an awesome light dinner that my boys absolutely love. For a more substantial meal, I'll cook up a double batch in a Dutch oven and serve it over rice for my big group.

SERVES 4

STIR-FRY SAUCE

3 tbsp (45 ml) low-sodium soy sauce

1 tbsp (15 g) finely grated ginger root

1 tbsp (15 ml) toasted sesame oil

1 tbsp (15 ml) rice vinegar

1 tbsp (15 ml) sriracha, or to taste

1 tbsp (9 g) brown sugar

1 tsp minced garlic

EGG ROLL FILLING

1 tbsp (15 ml) vegetable oil

1 lb (450 g) 80% lean ground pork or beef

½ tsp salt, or to taste

Freshly ground black pepper, to taste

½ cup (55 g) seeded and diced red bell pepper

½ cup (65 g) coarsely shredded carrot

1 (10-oz [280-g]) bag tri-color coleslaw mix

2 green onions, thinly sliced

2 tbsp (6 g) finely chopped fresh mint, optional

2 tbsp (30 g) sesame seeds, or as needed

FOR SERVING

1 head of butter lettuce, separated into individual leaves

Sweet chili sauce, optional (I like Mae Ploy™)

In a small bowl, combine the soy sauce, ginger, sesame oil, vinegar, sriracha, brown sugar and garlic to make the stir-fry sauce. Set it aside.

Add the vegetable oil to a deep 14-inch (35-cm) skillet or sauté pan, and place it over medium heat. Add the pork and cook, stirring to break up the meat, for 4 to 5 minutes or until browned. Drain off the excess grease, return the skillet to the heat and season the pork with the salt and pepper.

Add the bell pepper and shredded carrot and cook, stirring, for 3 to 4 minutes, until slightly softened. Add the coleslaw mix, green onions and the stir-fry sauce. Cook, stirring, for 2 to 3 minutes more, until the cabbage is wilted and the carrots and bell pepper are fork-tender. Remove the skillet from the heat and stir in the mint, if using. Taste and season with additional salt and pepper, if needed, and sprinkle on the sesame seeds.

To serve, fold 2 to 3 tablespoons (20 to 30 g) of the egg roll filling inside a lettuce leaf and garnish it with a drizzle of sweet chili sauce, if desired.

CAJUN BARBECUE RIBS

Your slow cooker makes easy work of these sticky, smoky, incredibly tender baby back ribs. The Kickin' Cajun Seasoning Mix in this recipe is one of my very favorite dry rubs, and combined with bottled barbecue sauce, it is an easy way to add tons of great flavor to these ribs.

This slow-cooker method is a great way to free up grill space when you're feeding a big group at a summer barbecue or to add the taste of summer to your menu any time of year. This mostly hands-off method requires a small amount of prep and a little bit of your time at the end to finish off the ribs under the broiler until they are nicely caramelized.

SERVES 4 TO 6

2 racks of pork baby back ribs, approximately 5 lbs (2.3 kg)

3 tbsp (27 g) Kickin' Cajun Seasoning Mix (page 184), or as needed

1 cup (240 ml) barbecue sauce, divided (I like Kinder's Mild BBQ Sauce)

Coat the insert of a 6-quart (5.5-L) slow cooker with nonstick cooking spray.

Cut each rack of ribs in half and pat them dry with paper towels. Transfer the ribs to a large sheet of foil, meaty side up. Sprinkle half of the Kickin' Cajun Seasoning Mix over the ribs and press it into the flesh of the ribs with your hands. Repeat on the back side of the ribs with the remaining seasoning mix.

Transfer the ribs to your slow cooker by placing them meaty side out against its walls, overlapping them as needed to fit. Cover and cook for 6 to 7 hours on low, until the ribs are very tender.

Preheat your oven to broil and transfer the cooked ribs, meaty side up, to a large baking sheet lined with a clean sheet of foil. Brush the ribs with half of the barbecue sauce and broil for 3 or 4 minutes, watching closely to be sure they don't burn. When the sauce is browned and nicely caramelized, remove the baking sheet from the oven. Brush the ribs with the remaining sauce and let them rest for 5 minutes.

Cut the ribs in between the bones before serving.

CAST-IRON SKILLET PIZZA TWO WAYS

If pizza night is a not a tradition in your home, this recipe just may change that. Most grocery stores carry convenient, one-pound (450 g) bags of pizza dough now, which means that making fresh, homemade pizza is even quicker than ordering out.

The pizza can be done with a delightfully crisp thin crust or with a thicker pan-style crust that can handle more substantial toppings. I'm including my recipe for a quick, no-cook pizza sauce, but you could opt for a jar of store-bought pizza or marinara sauce, which is easy to keep on hand for pizza night. These pizzas are easy to customize with your family's favorite toppings, but for a simply delicious choice, give my Pepperoni-Mushroom Pizza or Three-Cheese Prosciutto and Basil Pizza (page 57) a try.

THICK-CRUST (PAN-STYLE) PEPPERONI-MUSHROOM PIZZA

YIELDS 1 (12" [30-CM]) PIZZA

1 lb (450 g) store-bought pizza dough

Olive oil, as needed

½ cup (120 ml) Easy No-Cook Pizza Sauce (page 57), or as needed

1 cup (120 g) shredded Italian cheese blend (I use a provolone, asiago, fontina and Parmesan blend)

½ cup (55 g) chopped green bell pepper

½ cup (40 g) sliced mushrooms

1 cup (120 g) shredded mozzarella cheese

12 slices of pepperoni

Preheat the oven to 475°F (250°C).

Remove the pizza dough from the packaging and let it sit on a floured board for 20 to 30 minutes. Meanwhile, lightly grease a 12-inch (30-cm) cast-iron skillet with olive oil.

Use a rolling pin to roll the dough out to be close to the size of your skillet. Transfer the dough to the skillet, and use your hands to stretch it to fit, pressing it slightly up the sides of the skillet. Spread the pizza sauce over the surface of the dough, leaving about a ¼-inch (5-mm) border around the edge. Top with the Italian cheese blend, sprinkle on the bell pepper and mushrooms, then top with the shredded mozzarella cheese and, finally, the pepperoni.

Transfer the skillet to the oven and bake for 15 minutes, until the edges of the crust are golden brown and the cheese is melted and bubbly.

Remove the skillet from the oven and allow it to sit for 3 to 5 minutes to cool slightly. Using pot holders and a spatula, carefully transfer the pizza to a cutting board, slice it and serve.

(continued)

THREE-CHEESE PROSCIUTTO AND BASIL THIN-CRUST PIZZA

YIELDS 2 (10" [25-CM]) PIZZAS

1 lb (450 g) store-bought pizza dough

Olive oil, as needed

½ cup (120 ml) Easy No-Cook Pizza Sauce, or as needed, divided

1½ cups (180 g) shredded provolone or Italian cheese blend, divided

1½ cups (180 g) shredded mozzarella cheese, divided

½ cup (90 g) shredded Parmesan cheese, divided

4 oz (115 g) thinly sliced prosciutto, divided

½ cup (20 g) chopped fresh basil

Preheat the oven to 475°F (250°C).

Remove the pizza dough from the packaging and let it sit on a floured board for 20 to 30 minutes. Meanwhile, lightly grease a 10-inch (25-cm) cast-iron skillet with olive oil.

Use a sharp knife to slice the dough in half as evenly as possible and set one half aside. Use a rolling pin to roll out the other half of the dough to be close to the size of your skillet. Transfer the dough to the skillet and use your hands to stretch it to fit, pressing it slightly up the sides of the skillet.

Top the dough with about ¼ cup (60 ml) of the pizza sauce (or as needed), and sprinkle it with ¾ cup (90 g) of shredded provolone, ¾ cup (90 g) of mozzarella and ¼ cup (45 g) of shredded Parmesan. Bake for 10 minutes and then remove the skillet from the oven. Tear half of the prosciutto into pieces and pile it on top of the melted cheese. Return the skillet to the oven and bake for an additional 3 to 5 minutes, until the edges of the pizza are golden brown and the cheese is bubbly.

Remove the skillet from the oven and allow it to sit for 3 to 5 minutes to cool slightly. Using potholders and a spatula, carefully lift the pizza from the skillet and transfer it to a cutting board. Top the pizza with fresh basil, slice it and serve.

To make the second pizza, roll out the second half of the pizza dough. When the skillet has cooled enough to handle, wipe it out with a paper towel, grease it lightly with additional olive oil and repeat the process with the remaining sauce, provolone, mozzarella, Parmesan, prosciutto and basil.

EASY NO-COOK PIZZA SAUCE
MAKES ABOUT 2 CUPS (480 ML)

1 (14.5-oz [410-g]) can diced tomatoes, undrained

1 (6-oz [170-g]) can tomato paste

1 tsp sugar

¾ tsp dried oregano

½ tsp dried basil

¼ tsp red pepper flakes, or to taste

Place the tomatoes, tomato paste, sugar, oregano, basil and red pepper flakes in the bowl of a food processor and pulse until smooth. Store in an airtight container in the refrigerator for up to 4 days.

VEGGIE-PACKED MEATLOAF WITH BARBECUE GLAZE

A variety of fresh veggies add color, texture and wonderful flavor to this tender slow-cooker meatloaf. I top it with a simple barbecue glaze, which locks in the kid-friendly nature of this meal. Enclosing the meatloaf with a foil bowl ensures easy cleanup and gives you something to hold on to when transferring the meatloaf in and out of the slow cooker. If you'd like to use this meatloaf specifically for sandwiches, I recommend making it a day in advance and refrigerating it overnight. It will set up and slice beautifully when chilled.

SERVES 6

MEATLOAF

2 large eggs

1 cup (70 g) crushed saltines (about 20 crackers)

1 cup (120 g) shredded cheddar cheese

½ cup (75 g) diced onion

½ cup (55 g) diced red bell pepper

½ cup (65 g) finely shredded carrot

½ cup (60 g) finely shredded zucchini

½ cup (70 g) frozen corn, thawed

¼ cup (60 ml) ketchup

¼ cup (60 ml) milk

1 tbsp (15 ml) Worcestershire sauce

1 tbsp (9 g) chili powder

½ tsp garlic powder

¼ tsp black pepper

2 lb (910 g) lean ground beef

BARBECUE GLAZE

¼ cup (60 ml) ketchup

¼ cup (60 ml) barbecue sauce (I like Kinder's Mild BBQ Sauce)

1 tbsp (15 g) packed brown sugar

1 tbsp (15 g) Dijon mustard

In a large bowl, lightly whisk the eggs. Add the saltines, cheddar cheese, onion, bell pepper, carrot, zucchini, corn, ketchup, milk, Worcestershire sauce, chili powder, garlic powder and black pepper. Crumble the ground beef over the mixture and mix until just combined.

Coat an 18 × 12-inch (45 × 30-cm) sheet of heavy-duty foil with nonstick cooking spray. Turn the meatloaf mixture out onto the foil and use your hands to form it into an oval loaf that's approximately 9 × 6 inches (23 × 15 cm). Fold the edges of the foil up and over to make a bowl around the meatloaf. Place it in the slow cooker. Cover and cook for 5 to 6 hours on low.

In a small bowl, combine the ketchup, barbecue sauce, brown sugar and mustard to make the glaze. When the cooking time is up, spread it over the meatloaf, then cover and continue to cook on low for about 30 to 45 minutes until the center of the meatloaf registers 160°F (70°C).

Carefully lift the foil bowl from the slow cooker and drain off the grease. Transfer the meatloaf to a cutting board or serving platter and let it rest for 10 minutes before slicing.

SMOKY CHIPOTLE SHREDDED BEEF

Chipotle peppers in adobo sauce add a distinctive and delicious smoky flavor to this versatile shredded beef. The spice in this dish is offset by a touch of cider vinegar and brown sugar, creating an irresistible flavor combination. I like to cook up some rice and set out a variety of toppings so we can make our own custom burrito bowls, but this beef is also excellent for a variety of Mexican entrées, from tacos to enchiladas to nachos and more!

SERVES 6 TO 8

1 (3½–4-lb [1.5–1.8-kg]) boneless beef chuck roast

1 cup (150 g) diced white onion

1 (14.5-oz [410-g]) can tomato sauce

1 (4-oz [115-g]) can mild diced green chiles, drained

2 tbsp (15 g) finely chopped chipotle peppers in adobo sauce, plus 1 tsp sauce

2 tbsp (30 ml) cider vinegar

2 tbsp (18 g) brown sugar

1 tbsp (9 g) ground cumin

2 tsp (6 g) minced garlic

1 tsp smoked paprika

1 tsp oregano

½ tsp salt

½ tsp freshly ground black pepper

3–4 cups (680–910 g) cooked rice, for serving

OPTIONAL TOPPINGS

Diced fresh tomato, thinly sliced green onion, chopped avocado, shredded cheese, cilantro, sour cream, salsa

Cut the chuck roast into four or five large chunks and trim the fat from the edges of the beef as best you can. Place the trimmed beef into a 6-quart (5.5-L) slow cooker and sprinkle it with the diced onion.

Whisk together the tomato sauce, chiles, chipotle peppers, vinegar, brown sugar, cumin, garlic, paprika, oregano, salt and black pepper in a small mixing bowl. Pour the mixture over the beef and toss the beef in the sauce to coat the pieces well. Cover and cook for 7 to 8 hours on low or 5 to 6 hours on high, until the beef is very tender and easy to shred. Transfer the cooked beef to a large bowl and allow it to rest.

Use two forks to shred the beef into the cooking sauce. Alternatively, you can transfer the beef to a bowl to shred it and add as much of the sauce as desired to control the consistency.

Serve over the cooked rice with your toppings of choice.

PULLED PORK WITH ROOT BEER BARBECUE SAUCE

Although this recipe screams old-fashioned summer barbecue, I absolutely love the rich, slightly sweet flavor of this root beer–based barbecue sauce all through the year. Your slow cooker makes easy work of turning a pork loin into incredibly tender pulled pork. This leaner cut allows you to make use of the entire piece of meat, eliminating the need to pick through and discard excess fat like you would with a pork shoulder or butt roast. It is delicious on toasted hamburger buns, rolled into tortillas or piled high on top of baked potatoes. Cooking this recipe on low yields amazingly tender shredded pork.

SERVES 6 TO 8

PULLED PORK

1 (3–3½-lb [1.3–1.6-kg]) whole boneless pork loin

1 tbsp (9 g) chili powder

1 tsp salt

½ tsp freshly ground black pepper

¾ cup (180 ml) root beer

ROOT BEER BARBECUE SAUCE

1½ cups (360 ml) root beer

1½ cups (360 ml) ketchup

⅓ cup (80 ml) orange juice

⅓ cup (80 ml) Worcestershire sauce

2 tbsp (30 ml) molasses

1 tbsp (9 g) brown sugar

1 tbsp (15 g) yellow mustard

1 tsp minced garlic

1 tsp liquid smoke

1 tsp onion powder

½ tsp freshly ground black pepper, or to taste

Salt, to taste

6–8 toasted hamburger buns, for serving

Cut the pork loin into four pieces and place them in a 6-quart (5.5-L) slow cooker. Sprinkle them with the chili powder, salt and pepper, then pour the root beer into the slow cooker around the pork. Cover and cook for 6 to 7 hours on low, until the pork is very tender and easy to shred.

Meanwhile, make the sauce by combining the root beer, ketchup, orange juice, Worcestershire sauce, molasses, brown sugar, mustard, garlic, liquid smoke, onion powder and pepper in a large, heavy saucepan and whisking until smooth. Bring the mixture to a boil over medium heat, stirring occasionally. Reduce the heat to medium-low and simmer for 8 to 10 minutes to blend the flavors and reduce the sauce slightly. Season to taste with salt, if you feel it needs it, and additional black pepper. Remove the pan from the heat. Allow the sauce to cool slightly, then transfer it to a bowl or other container with a tight-fitting lid and refrigerate it until you're ready to use it. The sauce can be made in advance and stored in an airtight container in the refrigerator for up to 1 week.

When the cooking time is up, remove the pork to a large cutting board and discard all but about ½ cup (120 ml) of the cooking liquid. Use two forks to shred the pork, then return it to the slow cooker with the reserved cooking liquid. Add as much of the Root Beer Barbecue Sauce as desired and toss with the shredded pork to combine. I usually add about ½ cup to 1 cup (120 to 240 ml) of the sauce and reserve the rest to serve on the side so people can make their sandwiches as saucy as they'd like.

Cover and cook on low for an additional 30 minutes, until warmed through. Serve on toasted hamburger buns with additional Root Beer Barbecue Sauce on the side.

SAUSAGE, CABBAGE AND POTATO SUPPER

With smoked sausage, sweet cabbage, creamy potatoes and carrots simmered in a simply seasoned broth, this all-in-one dish cooks up in nothing flat. It's just the thing to warm up your family on a cold winter evening. I always serve it with warm slices of French bread slathered with butter to soak up the flavorful broth.

SERVES 6

2 tbsp (30 ml) olive oil

24 oz (910 g) fully cooked smoked sausage, sliced into 1" (3-cm) pieces

1 cup (150 g) roughly chopped red onion

1½ lbs (675 g) baby red and Yukon Gold potatoes, halved

3 carrots, peeled and roughly chopped

1 tsp minced garlic

1 tsp all-purpose seasoning (I like Lawry's Seasoned Salt)

½ tsp paprika

½ tsp freshly ground black pepper

2 cups (480 ml) low-sodium chicken broth (I like Better Than Bouillon)

1 medium head of cabbage, chopped

2 tbsp (28 g) butter, cut into small pats

Crusty French bread, for serving

Add the olive oil to a large Dutch oven and place it over medium heat. Add the sausage and onion and cook for 5 minutes, stirring frequently, until the sausage is lightly browned and the onion is tender. Add the potatoes, carrots, garlic, all-purpose seasoning, paprika and pepper, and cook, stirring, for another 2 to 3 minutes. Add the broth, then cover and cook on low for 20 minutes, until the vegetables are just barely tender when pierced with a sharp knife.

Add the cabbage, cover and cook for another 10 minutes, until the vegetables are perfectly fork-tender. Remove the cover and top with pats of butter. Cover for 1 to 2 minutes to melt the butter.

Ladle into bowls and serve with slices of crusty French bread on the side for dipping.

PASTA

Donuts aside, pasta is easily my husband's biggest weakness. As a result, I've cooked a whole lot of pasta dishes over time and adapted many to either the slow-cooker or one-pot method of preparation.

Classic Italian flavors are front and center in the meltingly tender Slow-Cooked Short Rib Ragù (page 70), which is utterly delicious served over pasta but also wonderful with mashed potatoes or polenta. My family would be completely content if the Lasagna Florentine with Tomato Cream Sauce (page 69) or the Creamy "Baked" Ziti (page 82) were on our menu every week. Be ahead of the game and cook up my Big-Batch Bolognese (page 81) on the weekend, freeze a portion and use the rest for a couple of easy meals during the week.

The one-pot method works so well for pasta dishes that I've included five favorites to choose from, including the Ground Beef Stroganoff Pasta Skillet (page 85), my nostalgic take on this classic dish. If you've got fans of peanut sauce in your house, they will love the vibrant and oh-so-tasty Easy Peanut Noodles with Chicken and Veggies (page 73). The one-pot Jambalaya Pasta (page 86) came about through my attempt to re-create one of my husband's favorite restaurant dishes at home, and I'm happy to say it is a winner of a dish! The Cheesy Taco Pasta Skillet (page 74) and Turkey-Vegetable Skillet Lasagna (page 78) will go over in a big way with your family and make your task of preparing dinner a breeze on crazy-busy days.

LASAGNA FLORENTINE WITH TOMATO CREAM SAUCE

This substantial lasagna is stacked high with layers of creamy ricotta cheese, spinach, mozzarella, Parmesan and a delicious beefy tomato cream sauce. Lasagna has always been one of the most requested meals in our house, and this slow-cooker version is one of our favorites. After the initial cooking time, the lasagna should rest for 20 to 30 minutes, which gives you just enough time to toss a salad and slice a loaf of French bread.

SERVES 6 TO 8

1 tbsp (15 ml) olive oil

1 lb (450 g) lean ground beef

½ cup (75 g) diced white or yellow onion

1 tsp minced garlic

2 tsp (2 g) Italian seasoning

½ tsp salt

Freshly ground black pepper, to taste

1 (24–26-oz [680–740-g]) jar marinara sauce

1 (8-oz [230-g]) can tomato sauce

¾ cup (180 ml) heavy cream

1 (10-oz [280-g]) package chopped frozen spinach, completely thawed

1 (15-oz [425-g]) container part-skim ricotta cheese

1 egg

9 uncooked lasagna noodles (not the no-boil variety)

2 cups (150 g) stemmed and sliced cremini (brown button) mushrooms

3 cups (360 g) shredded mozzarella cheese, divided

½ cup (90 g) grated Parmesan cheese, divided

2 tbsp (6 g) chopped Italian parsley

Pour the olive oil into a 12-inch (30-cm) skillet and place it over medium heat. Add the ground beef and onion and cook for 4 to 5 minutes, breaking up the beef until it is no longer pink. Drain off as much of the grease from the skillet as possible and return it to the heat. Add the garlic, Italian seasoning, salt and pepper, and cook for another 2 minutes. Add the marinara sauce, tomato sauce and heavy cream, reduce the heat to low and allow the mixture to simmer for 5 minutes.

Meanwhile, place the thawed spinach between a double layer of paper towels. Fold the paper towels over to enclose the spinach and wring it out with your hands over the sink to drain off as much of the liquid as possible. Transfer the drained spinach to a small mixing bowl and add the ricotta and egg. Mix it well and set it aside.

Spray the bottom and sides of a 6-quart (5.5-L) slow-cooker insert with nonstick cooking spray.

Add approximately 1 cup (240 ml) of the meat sauce to the slow cooker and use a spoon to spread it out to cover the bottom. Place one lasagna noodle down the center over the meat sauce. Break two more lasagna noodles in half and place them as needed to completely cover the meat sauce. Dollop half of the ricotta mixture over the noodles and scatter half of the mushrooms over the top. Sprinkle with one-third of the shredded mozzarella and Parmesan cheeses, and cover with one-third of the remaining meat sauce. Repeat to create one more layer.

End with one last layer of three lasagna noodles, the remaining meat sauce and the remaining mozzarella and Parmesan cheeses.

Cover and cook on low for 3 to 4 hours, until the noodles are tender and the edges of the lasagna are beginning to brown. Turn the slow cooker off and allow the lasagna to rest, covered, for 20 to 30 minutes. Top with fresh parsley and slice it into serving-size portions.

SLOW-COOKED SHORT RIB RAGÙ

The slow cooker is an excellent choice for creating this melt-in-your-mouth short rib ragù. After a quick turn in a skillet, beef short ribs are cooked in a rich, robust sauce made with Italian tomatoes, red wine and flavorful herbs. Start with boneless ribs, and at the end of the cooking time you can shred the meat right into the luscious sauce. This recipe involves a little bit of prep to develop a more complex flavor, but it all pays off in the end. This meaty, stick-to-your ribs ragù is excellent served over a substantial pasta like pappardelle or rigatoni and is equally delicious served over polenta or creamy mashed potatoes.

SERVES 6 TO 8

2½ lbs (1.2 kg) boneless beef short ribs

1½ tsp (5 g) salt, divided

Freshly ground black pepper

2 tbsp (30 ml) olive oil

½ cup (65 g) diced carrot (about 1 large carrot)

½ cup diced celery (about 1 celery rib)

½ cup (75 g) diced yellow onion

¼ tsp red pepper flakes, or to taste

1 tsp chopped garlic

2 tbsp (20 g) tomato paste

½ cup (120 ml) robust, full-bodied red wine (like cabernet sauvignon, zinfandel, syrah or merlot)

¾ cup (180 ml) low-sodium beef broth

1 (28-oz [800-g]) can crushed tomatoes (preferably San Marzano)

1 tsp dried thyme

1 tsp rosemary

½ tsp dried oregano

1 bay leaf

2 tbsp (6 g) freshly chopped parsley

1 lb (450 g) pappardelle or rigatoni pasta

¼ cup (50 g) Parmesan cheese, plus more for serving

Cut the short ribs in half and season with 1 teaspoon of salt and a generous amount of pepper.

Heat the olive oil in a large pot or Dutch oven over medium-high heat. Brown the seasoned short ribs for 2 minutes per side, then transfer them to the slow cooker.

Reduce the heat under the pot to medium and add the carrot, celery, onion, red pepper flakes and garlic to the meat drippings. Season with the remaining ½ teaspoon of salt and more pepper. Sauté until the veggies are just barely tender, about 3 minutes. Stir the tomato paste into the veggies, then add the red wine and broth. Increase the heat to medium-high and stir, scraping up the browned bits from the bottom of the pot. Bring the mixture to a low boil, remove the pot from the heat and pour the mixture over the short ribs in the slow cooker.

Add the crushed tomatoes, thyme, rosemary and oregano and stir everything together. Tuck a bay leaf into the mixture, cover and cook for 6 to 8 hours on low or for 3 to 4 hours on high, until the short ribs are fork-tender and easy to shred.

Turn off the slow cooker and remove and discard the bay leaf. Skim and discard the excess grease from the sauce by pressing the back of a large spoon lightly against the surface of the sauce in several places, allowing grease to pool into the spoon. Use two forks to shred the meat into the sauce. Stir in the parsley.

Cook the pasta of your choice according to the package directions. Drain the cooked pasta and return it to the still-warm empty pot. Add as much of the ragù as needed. Toss with the Parmesan cheese and serve with extra Parmesan on the side.

Leftovers will stay fresh for 3 to 4 days if stored in an airtight container in the refrigerator or for several months if frozen.

EASY PEANUT NOODLES WITH CHICKEN AND VEGGIES

Anything I top with peanut sauce is a hit with my group, and this noodle dish is no exception. It is delicious served slightly warm or after it has chilled in the refrigerator. Vibrant veggies and chopped peanuts add both color and texture and make it a beautiful dish to serve at a potluck buffet. To save time, the Easy Peanut Sauce can be prepared several days in advance and stored for up to a week in the refrigerator.

SERVES 6

EASY PEANUT SAUCE

½ cup (90 g) creamy peanut butter

2 tbsp (30 ml) low-sodium soy sauce

2 tbsp (30 ml) honey

2 tbsp (30 ml) unseasoned rice vinegar

½ lime, juiced

2 tsp (10 g) peeled and finely grated ginger root or ¾ tsp ground ginger

½ tsp minced garlic

¼ tsp curry powder

¼ tsp red pepper flakes, or to taste

⅓ cup (80 ml) warm water, or as needed to reach desired consistency

NOODLES

12 oz (345 g) spaghetti or lo mein noodles

1 tbsp (15 ml) toasted sesame oil

2 tbsp (30 ml) vegetable oil

1 large red bell pepper, seeded and thinly sliced

2 cups (350 g) chopped broccoli florets

1 tsp minced garlic

1½ cups (225 g) shredded carrot

2 cups (250 g) chopped All-Purpose Chicken (page 41) or rotisserie chicken breast

3 green onions, thinly sliced

GARNISH

⅓ cup (15 g) chopped fresh cilantro

¼ cup (30 g) chopped peanuts

1 tbsp (15 g) sesame seeds

Place the peanut butter, soy sauce, honey, vinegar, lime juice, ginger, garlic, curry powder and red pepper flakes in the bowl of a blender or food processor. With the motor running, slowly pour the water through the feed tube a little a time, until the mixture reaches the desired consistency. You want it thin enough to pour, but not watery. Set it aside, or if making the sauce in advance, transfer it to an airtight container (a small mason jar works perfectly) and store it in the refrigerator for up to a week.

Cook the noodles according to the package directions in a Dutch oven. Transfer the cooked noodles to a colander to drain, toss them with the sesame oil and set it aside. Pour all the water out of the pot and wipe it dry with a towel.

Add the vegetable oil to the pot and place it over medium-high heat. Add the bell pepper and broccoli and sauté for 2 to 3 minutes, until slightly tender. Add the garlic and shredded carrot and continue to cook for another 1 to 2 minutes, until the garlic is fragrant and the veggies are fork-tender. Add the chicken to the pot along with the cooked pasta, Easy Peanut Sauce and the green onions. Use tongs to toss the mixture until the noodles are evenly coated, adding a splash or two of water to loosen it up, if necessary.

Garnish with cilantro, peanuts and sesame seeds before serving.

CHEESY TACO PASTA SKILLET

This is hands-down one of the quickest, easiest recipes in my collection. It's a variation of a casserole I've made for ages that I've modified to take place all in one pan on the stove in about 30 minutes from start to finish. The familiar Mexican flavors make it a great family-friendly choice. Instead of purchasing a packet of taco seasoning from the grocery store, make a batch of my homemade mix and keep it on hand for all your Mexican-inspired dishes.

SERVES 6

1 lb (450 g) lean ground beef

½ cup (75 g) chopped onion

1 tsp minced garlic

2 tbsp (18 g) Flavor Fiesta Taco Seasoning Mix (page 184) or store-bought taco seasoning

2 cups (480 ml) low-sodium chicken broth (I like Better Than Bouillon)

1 (14.5-oz [410-g]) can diced tomatoes, undrained

1 (8-oz [230-g]) can tomato sauce

1 (15-oz [425-g]) can black beans, rinsed and drained

1 (4-oz [115-g]) can mild diced green chiles

8 oz (225 g) uncooked short dry pasta, like fusilli, rotelli, elbows or penne

1 cup (145 g) frozen corn

1 cup (120 g) shredded Monterey Jack cheese, divided

1 cup (120 g) shredded cheddar cheese, divided

GARNISH

¼ cup (45 g) sliced black olives

¼ cup (10 g) chopped cilantro

3 green onions, thinly sliced

Sour cream, optional

Place a large deep skillet or sauté pan with a lid over medium heat and add the ground beef, onion and garlic. Cook for 5 to 6 minutes, stirring to break up the meat, until browned. Drain off as much of the excess grease from the skillet as possible and return it to the heat. Add the Flavor Fiesta Taco Seasoning Mix and stir to combine it well with the beef. Add the broth, tomatoes, tomato sauce, black beans, chiles and pasta. Bring the mixture to a boil, then reduce the heat to low, cover and cook for 15 minutes.

Remove the cover, stir in the corn and simmer for an additional 3 to 4 minutes, until the sauce has been mostly absorbed.

Turn the heat off and stir in half of the Monterey Jack and cheddar cheeses. Sprinkle the remaining cheese over the top, and cover the skillet for 2 to 3 minutes, until the cheese has melted. Top with black olives, cilantro and green onions.

Garnish individual servings with sour cream, if desired.

CHICKEN CACCIATORE

Bone-in chicken thighs cook low and slow in a tomato-based sauce infused with garlic and Italian herbs. Get this classic Italian dish going in your slow cooker on a cold fall or winter lazy Sunday afternoon.

As with many of my recipes that feature canned tomatoes as one of the main flavor components, I highly recommend you use San Marzano tomatoes. They are milder, sweeter and less acidic than other canned tomato products and a better choice for recipes like this one.

SERVES 4

2 tbsp (30 ml) olive oil

1 carrot, peeled and diced

1 cup (150 g) diced onion

2 tsp (6 g) minced garlic

2 tbsp (20 g) tomato paste

2 tsp (2 g) dried oregano

1 tsp dried basil

¼ tsp red pepper flakes, or to taste

¼ tsp salt

Freshly ground black pepper, to taste

½ cup (120 ml) dry white wine, like sauvignon blanc, pinot grigio or chardonnay

8 bone-in chicken thighs, skin removed

1 (28-oz [800-g]) can crushed San Marzano tomatoes

8 oz (225 g) cremini mushrooms, quartered

2 tbsp (6 g) chopped Italian parsley

Shredded Parmesan cheese, for garnish

2 cups (455 g) cooked rice or 8 oz (230 g) cooked pasta

Drizzle the olive oil into a 12-inch (30-cm) skillet and place it over medium heat. Add the carrot, onion and garlic and sauté for 4 or 5 minutes, until the carrot and onion have just softened. Add the tomato paste, oregano, basil, red pepper flakes, salt and black pepper, and stir the mixture. Allow it to cook for 1 to 2 minutes to toast the spices. Add the wine and bring the mixture to a simmer.

Place the chicken in the slow cooker. Spoon the mixture from the skillet over the chicken and add the crushed tomatoes. Cover and cook on low for 4 to 5 hours, just until the chicken is tender and cooked through. Stir in the mushrooms and parsley, cover and continue to cook for an additional 30 to 60 minutes on low, just until the mushrooms have softened.

Garnish individual servings with plenty of shredded Parmesan cheese, and serve over rice or pasta.

TURKEY-VEGETABLE SKILLET LASAGNA

The first time I made a skillet lasagna it was truly a revelation. Lasagna is an often-requested dish in my house, but on those days when I just don't have the time or energy to go to the trouble, this quick and easy one-pot dish comes to the rescue. My turkey and veggie version is an attempt to lighten up what is typically a heavy meal. It still packs all the flavor and comfort of classic lasagna but is a bit less guilt-inducing.

SERVES 6

2 tbsp (30 ml) olive oil

1 lb (450 g) lean ground turkey

½ cup (65 g) diced carrot

½ cup (75 g) diced onion

½ tsp salt, or to taste

Freshly ground black pepper, to taste

1 cup (150 g) chopped zucchini

1 cup (75 g) chopped mushrooms

1 tsp minced garlic

1 tsp Italian seasoning

8 curly-edged lasagna noodles (not the no-boil variety), each broken into 3 or 4 pieces

½ cup (120 ml) water

1 (14.5-oz [410-g]) can diced tomatoes, undrained

1 (25-oz [710-g]) jar marinara sauce

1 cup (120 g) part-skim ricotta cheese

1½ cups (180 g) shredded mozzarella cheese

⅓ cup (60 g) grated Parmesan cheese

½ cup (20 g) chopped fresh basil, for serving

Heat the olive oil in a deep 12- to 14-inch (30- to 35-cm) sauté pan with a lid over medium heat. When the oil is hot, add the ground turkey, carrot and onion and cook for about 5 to 6 minutes, breaking up the ground turkey with a spoon, until no pink remains. Drain off as much of the grease as you can, and return the skillet to the stove. Season the meat with the salt and pepper. Add the zucchini, mushrooms, garlic and Italian seasoning. Continue to cook for about 3 to 4 minutes more, stirring occasionally.

Place the uncooked broken lasagna noodles over the turkey and vegetable mixture to cover it completely. Pour the water, tomatoes and marinara sauce evenly over the pasta, using the back of a spoon to smooth it out, making sure that the edges of the pasta are covered with sauce. Bring the mixture to a good simmer, then reduce the heat to medium-low, cover the pan and simmer for 25 minutes.

Remove the cover and drop small dollops of the ricotta over the surface of the lasagna and sprinkle on the mozzarella and Parmesan cheeses. Cover the pan and cook for an additional 5 minutes, until the ricotta is warmed and the mozzarella has melted. Sprinkle with fresh basil and serve.

BIG-BATCH BOLOGNESE

What's better than coming home to a pot of comforting Bolognese bubbling away in your slow cooker? This recipe requires a little work to get it started, but the upside is that it makes a whopping three quarts (3 L) of versatile meat sauce good for a variety of purposes. Use what you need for dinner and freeze the rest for a couple of easy meals in the coming weeks. This sauce is requested over and over again by my pasta-loving family.

YIELDS APPROXIMATELY 3 QUARTS (3 L)

¼ cup (60 ml) olive oil, divided

1 small white or yellow onion, diced

2 carrots, finely diced

2 celery ribs, finely diced

½ cup (20 g) chopped fresh parsley

1 tbsp (9 g) minced garlic

2 tsp (10 g) salt, divided, or to taste

1 (6-oz [170-g]) can tomato paste

1 lb (450 g) ground beef (80–85% lean)

1 lb (450 g) ground pork (80% lean)

Freshly ground black pepper

1 cup (240 ml) whole milk

1 cup (240 ml) wine (a good hearty red like cabernet sauvignon or zinfandel, or a dry white like sauvignon blanc or pinot grigio)

2 (28-oz [800-g]) cans good-quality crushed Italian tomatoes (preferably San Marzano)

1 cup (240 ml) low-sodium beef broth

1 tbsp (2 g) dried thyme

1 tbsp (2 g) dried oregano

2 tsp (2 g) dried basil

¼ tsp ground nutmeg

12–16 oz (340–455 g) dry pasta of your choice, for serving

Finely grated Parmesan cheese, for garnish

Pour 2 tablespoons (30 ml) of olive oil into a deep 14-inch (35-cm) skillet or braising pan and place it over medium heat. Add the onion, carrot and celery, and cook, stirring occasionally, for about 3 or 4 minutes, until the vegetables have softened but not browned. Add the parsley, garlic, ½ teaspoon of salt and the tomato paste. Stir the mixture well and simmer it for 1 to 2 minutes. Transfer the mixture to a 6-quart (5.5-L) slow cooker.

Add the remaining 2 tablespoons (30 ml) of olive oil to the empty skillet and place it over medium heat. Add the ground beef and ground pork. Season the meat with black pepper and 1 teaspoon of salt. Cook for about 5 to 6 minutes, stirring to break up the meat, until no pink remains. Drain the grease from the skillet, return it to the heat and add the milk. Cook and stir for 5 or 6 minutes, until the milk has almost completely been absorbed by the meat. Add the wine and simmer again for an additional 2 to 3 minutes to slightly reduce the sauce. Transfer the mixture to the slow cooker.

Add the crushed tomatoes, broth, thyme, oregano, basil, nutmeg, ½ teaspoon of salt and more pepper to the slow cooker. Stir well. Cover and cook for 5 to 7 hours on low.

When ready to serve, cook the pasta according to the package directions, drain it and return it to the warm pasta pot. Add the desired amount of the Bolognese, and toss to combine it well. Stir in a good amount of grated Parmesan cheese before serving.

CREAMY "BAKED" ZITI

You would never guess how effortless this luscious dish is to prepare. Uncooked pasta is layered with cooked ground beef and a simple but delicious blend of spices. Your favorite store-bought marinara tops it off. Dollops of ricotta cheese, shredded mozzarella and Parmesan are added toward the end of the cooking time and quickly melt down over this glorious casserole.

Watching the cooking time closely is the key to success with slow-cooker pasta recipes. Be ready to check on the dish near the lower end of the suggested time range.

SERVES 6

2 tbsp (30 ml) olive oil

1 lb (450 g) lean ground beef

1 cup (150 g) diced onion

2 tsp (6 g) minced garlic

2 tsp (2 g) Italian seasoning

½ tsp fennel seeds, lightly crushed

½ tsp salt

¼ tsp red pepper flakes, optional

12 oz (340 g) uncooked ziti or penne

1 (24-26-oz [710-770-ml]) jar marinara sauce

1 (14.5-oz [410-g]) can diced tomatoes, undrained

½ cup (120 ml) water

¾ cup (90 g) ricotta cheese

¼ cup (45 g) finely shredded Parmesan cheese, plus more for garnish

2 tbsp (6 g) minced fresh Italian parsley, plus more for garnish

1 cup (120 g) shredded mozzarella cheese

Pour the olive oil into a 12-inch (30-cm) skillet and place it over medium heat. Add the ground beef, onion and garlic, and cook for about 5 to 6 minutes, stirring to break up the beef, until crumbly and browned with no pink remaining. Drain off the grease from the skillet and return it to the heat. Add the Italian seasoning, fennel seeds, salt and red pepper flakes, and cook, stirring, for another 1 to 2 minutes, until fragrant. Transfer the mixture to a 6-quart (5.5-L) slow cooker.

Add the pasta in an even layer over the beef mixture.

Combine the marinara sauce, tomatoes and water in a medium bowl, and pour the mixture over the pasta, being sure the pasta is completely immersed in liquid. Use the back of a spoon to spread the sauce out if needed. Cover the slow cooker and cook on low for 2 hours, until the pasta is just barely al dente. Watch closely to prevent the pasta from becoming too soft.

At the end of the cooking time, combine the ricotta, Parmesan cheese and parsley in a small bowl. Remove the slow-cooker's cover and stir the pasta to combine it well with the meat and sauce. Sprinkle the mozzarella cheese over the pasta mixture, and dollop small spoonfuls of the ricotta mixture over the top of the mozzarella. Cover and cook on low for an additional 20 to 25 minutes, just until the cheese mixture is warm and has melted down.

Garnish with additional Parmesan cheese and parsley, if desired, before serving.

GROUND BEEF STROGANOFF PASTA SKILLET

Ground beef stroganoff was a regular on our menu when Paul and I were a young couple just starting out on our own. It was a value-conscious version of classic beef stroganoff that suited both our tastes and our budget perfectly. I've carried that recipe forward to today and adapted it into a one-pot meal by adding dry pasta directly into the skillet to cook along with the other ingredients. It's now a fast and easy, super comforting dish that takes me back to a simpler time.

SERVES 6

2 tbsp (30 ml) olive oil, divided

1 lb (450 g) lean ground beef

1½ tsp (8 g) salt, divided

1 tsp freshly ground black pepper, divided

8 oz (225 g) white button mushrooms, quartered

¼ cup (60 ml) dry sherry or dry white wine, like sauvignon blanc or pinot grigio

1 cup (150 g) diced yellow onion

1 carrot, peeled and diced

2 tsp (6 g) minced garlic

1 tsp dried thyme

1 tsp paprika

2 tbsp (20 g) tomato paste

3½ cups (840 ml) low-sodium beef broth

1 tbsp (15 ml) Worcestershire sauce

2 tsp (10 g) Dijon mustard

6 oz (170 g) dry wide egg noodles

1 tbsp (10 g) cornstarch

2 tbsp (30 ml) water

⅓ cup (80 ml) sour cream

2 tbsp (6 g) chopped fresh Italian parsley

Add 1 tablespoon (15 ml) of olive oil to a large, deep skillet or braising pan with a lid and place it over medium-high heat. Add the ground beef, 1 teaspoon of salt and ½ teaspoon of black pepper. Cook, breaking the beef into small pieces with a spoon, until browned, about 5 minutes. Use a slotted spoon to transfer the cooked beef to a plate. Add the mushrooms to the drippings in the skillet and cook, stirring, for 1 to 2 minutes. Add the sherry and cook, stirring to scrape up any browned bits from the bottom of the skillet. Cook for 2 to 3 minutes, until the wine has mostly evaporated and the mushrooms have softened. Transfer the cooked mushrooms to the plate with the beef and set it aside.

Reduce the heat to medium and add the remaining 1 tablespoon (15 ml) of oil to the skillet. Add the onion, carrot, garlic, thyme, paprika and the remaining ½ teaspoons of salt and pepper, and cook until the carrots have softened and the onion is lightly browned, about 5 minutes. Stir the tomato paste into the vegetables. Add the broth, Worcestershire sauce and Dijon mustard to the skillet and stir to combine the mixture well. Bring it to a simmer and stir in the uncooked dry pasta. Cover and cook for 7 minutes, just until the noodles are al dente.

Combine the cornstarch with the water in a small bowl, stir it into the skillet along with the reserved beef and mushrooms and cook for 3 to 4 minutes, uncovered, until slightly thickened and heated through. Stir in the sour cream and parsley, and continue to simmer until the mixture is warmed through. Remove from the heat and let sit for 5 minutes before serving.

JAMBALAYA PASTA

This is my home-cooked version of one of my husband's favorite dishes from a local restaurant chain. Chicken, sausage and shrimp simmer in a creamy Cajun-spiced sauce with bell peppers, onion and garlic to create the classic flavors of jambalaya. Dry pasta is added and cooks up perfectly al dente. If you want to go mild, I recommend using smoked sausage, and to kick it up a notch, go with spicy andouille.

SERVES 6

2 tbsp (30 ml) olive oil

1 lb (450 g) boneless, skinless chicken breast, cut into bite-size pieces

½ lb (225 g) fully-cooked andouille or smoked sausage, cut on the diagonal into 1" (3-cm) thick pieces

1 cup (150 g) diced yellow onion

1 cup (110 g) chopped red or yellow bell pepper, or both

¼ cup (10 g) chopped fresh Italian parsley, plus more for garnish

1 tbsp plus 1 tsp (11 g) Kickin' Cajun Seasoning Mix (page 184) or store-bought Cajun seasoning, divided

2 tsp (6 g) minced garlic

1 (14.5-oz [410-g]) can diced tomatoes, undrained

2 cups (480 ml) low-sodium chicken broth (I like Better Than Bouillon)

8 oz (225 g) dry linguine or spaghetti

8–10 oz (225–280 g) raw shrimp (31–40 count), peeled, deveined and tails removed

½ cup (120 ml) heavy cream

Salt and freshly ground black pepper, to taste

Pour the olive oil into a Dutch oven and place it over medium-high heat. When the oil is hot, add the chicken, sausage, onion, bell pepper, parsley and 1 tablespoon (9 g) of Cajun seasoning. Sauté for 3 to 4 minutes, until the chicken and sausage are nicely seared. Add the garlic and sauté for 1 to 2 minutes.

Add the tomatoes, broth, remaining 1 teaspoon of the Cajun seasoning and the uncooked dry pasta, breaking the noodles in half if necessary to fit in the pan. Bring the mixture to a boil, then reduce the heat, cover and simmer for 10 minutes.

Remove the cover and add the shrimp and cream, stirring well to combine. Cover and continue to cook for an additional 5 minutes, until the shrimp is pinkish-orange and no longer opaque and the pasta is cooked al dente. Season with salt and freshly ground black pepper, and garnish with additional chopped fresh parsley, if desired.

SOUPS, STEWS AND CHILIS

This chapter is filled with year-round favorites that are cooked with little preparation throughout the day in your slow cooker or quickly and easily on your stovetop. They are all great busy-day options, and I love how easy these recipes make it to incorporate wholesome beans and fresh vegetables in a way that appeals to family members of all ages.

You'll find that many of these recipes are great for entertaining and work just as well at a summer barbecue as they do on a chilly fall evening. Serve the Beefy Game-Day Beer Chili (page 99) right out of your slow cooker for your next gathering, or add substance to your menu when you've got a crowd to feed with the Hearty Tex-Mex Chicken Chili (page 96). On those crazy-busy days, take advantage of the one-pot Chicken Parmesan Soup with Crumbled Croutons (page 100) that's ready in 30 minutes or less.

Some of these recipes require pureeing, and using an immersion blender is the quickest, easiest way to do this—it eliminates the messy step of transferring the contents to a countertop blender. If you must use a countertop blender, puree in batches and make sure the blender is never more than two-thirds full, as hot liquids may expand and leak out of the top.

These recipes freeze well, and to save space, I transfer the completely cooled food into zippered gallon-size plastic storage bags. I push out the excess air before closing the bags, then lay them flat and freeze them solid. The bags can then be stacked to save space. To reheat, thaw the bags in the refrigerator overnight, then warm the contents on the stove over medium heat or in the microwave.

BUSY-DAY ITALIAN VEGETABLE BEEF SOUP

Loaded with chunks of tender beef, veggies, beans and pasta, this hearty soup is truly a meal in itself. The use of precut beef stew meat and frozen mixed vegetables eliminates the usual slicing and dicing involved with many vegetable soup recipes, making it a great choice for those days when you don't have time to deal with much recipe prep in the morning. Considering the simplicity of the ingredients and the ease of preparation, this soup has a surprising depth of flavor and really hits the spot to satisfy my soup cravings.

SERVES 6

2 lbs (910 g) beef stew meat, cut into ½" (1-cm) pieces

6 cups (1.4 L) low-sodium beef broth

1 (14.5-oz [410-g]) can diced tomatoes, undrained

1 tsp dried Italian seasoning

½ tsp all-purpose seasoning (I like Lawry's Seasoned Salt)

½ tsp freshly ground black pepper, plus more to taste

2 cups (290 g) frozen mixed vegetables

1 (16-oz [455-g]) can cannellini or Great Northern beans, rinsed and drained

1 cup (116 g) uncooked elbow pasta

2 tbsp (6 g) chopped fresh Italian parsley

Salt, to taste

Shredded Parmesan cheese, for serving

Combine the beef, broth, tomatoes, Italian seasoning, all-purpose seasoning and pepper in a 6-quart (5.5-L) slow cooker. Stir to combine the ingredients. Cover and cook for 7 hours on low or for 5 hours on high, until the beef is fork-tender.

Stir in the frozen mixed vegetables, beans, pasta and parsley. Cover and continue cooking on low for 30 to 45 minutes, until the pasta is tender. Taste and season with salt and additional pepper as needed.

Ladle the soup into bowls and set out some shredded Parmesan cheese for topping.

Stored in an airtight container, this soup will keep well in the refrigerator for several days or freezer for 2 to 3 months.

CURRIED BUTTERNUT SQUASH-APPLE SOUP

Nothing screams fall more than a slow cooker full of this cozy soup. Apple and carrot add a sweet flavor that is enhanced by the warm spice of curry and garam masala. Things get silky and down-right luscious with the addition of coconut milk at the end of the cooking time. It's wonderful served with grilled cheese sandwiches for dunking.

You can get this soup started in nothing flat with the help of a package of peeled, cubed butternut squash, available in the produce section of most grocery stores. Eliminating the need to prepare the squash, they're a fantastic timesaver.

SERVES 4 TO 6

1 (20-oz [560-g]) package peeled, cubed butternut squash (approximately 4 cups)

1 crisp-sweet apple (like Honeycrisp), peeled, cored and coarsely chopped

½ cup (65 g) peeled, diced carrot

½ cup (75 g) diced shallot

2 tbsp (20 g) light brown sugar, plus more to taste

2 tsp (6 g) curry, plus more to taste

1 tsp garam masala, plus more to taste

¼ tsp salt, plus more to taste

2½ cups (600 ml) low-sodium chicken or vegetable broth

¾ cup (180 ml) unsweetened coconut milk

OPTIONAL TOPPINGS

Nonfat plain Greek yogurt or sour cream, chopped fresh chives

Add the squash, apple, carrot, shallot, brown sugar, curry, garam masala and salt to a 5- to 6-quart (4.7- to 5.5-L) slow cooker and stir to combine. Add the broth, cover and cook for 6 to 8 hours on low or 3 to 4 hours on high, until the squash and apple are tender.

Power off and unplug the slow cooker. Add the coconut milk and use an immersion blender to puree the mixture until smooth and creamy. Alternatively, transfer the soup to a blender in batches to puree it, then return it to the slow cooker.

Taste and add more brown sugar, curry, garam masala and salt as needed. Mix the soup again briefly to combine.

Serve it garnished with a dollop of Greek yogurt or sour cream and chopped fresh chives, if desired.

> **TIP:** This recipe can be doubled to use an entire 14-ounce (400-g) can of coconut milk. If you'd like to peel, seed and cube your own squash, you will need approximately 3 pounds (1.4 kg) of whole butternut squash to yield 4 cups (560 g) of 1-inch (3-cm) cubes.

CREAMY TOMATO-TORTELLINI SOUP

This comforting soup has been deemed a favorite by my son Connor and husband, Paul. It's reminiscent of the cream of tomato soup so many of us grew up eating with our grilled cheese sandwiches, but the flavors are far more complex in this made-from-scratch version. The addition of cheese tortellini and fresh basil make it a soup worthy of main-dish status.

Adding half-and-half or cream to tomato-based soups helps immensely to cut some of the acidic taste, but a key step for a good result is starting with high-quality San Marzano tomatoes. They are milder, sweeter and less acidic than other varieties and will yield a fabulous soup.

SERVES 6 TO 8

1 cup (150 g) diced sweet yellow onion

½ cup (65 g) peeled and diced carrot

1 tsp minced garlic

2 (28-oz [800-g]) cans whole, peeled San Marzano tomatoes, undrained

3 cups (720 ml) low-sodium vegetable or chicken broth

1 tsp sugar

1 tsp dried oregano

½ tsp salt, or to taste

¼ tsp freshly ground black pepper

2 bay leaves

½ cup (120 ml) half-and-half or heavy cream

¼ cup (45 g) shredded Parmesan cheese, plus more for serving

1 (20-oz [560-g]) package refrigerated cheese tortellini

½ cup (20 g) thinly sliced fresh basil leaves

Place the onion, carrot, garlic, tomatoes and their liquid, broth, sugar, oregano, salt, pepper and bay leaves into the insert of a 6-quart (5.5-L) slow cooker. Stir to combine the ingredients well, then cover and cook for 7 to 8 hours on low or 3 to 4 hours on high.

Power off and unplug the slow cooker. Remove and discard the bay leaves and use an immersion blender to blend the mixture until it is smooth. Alternatively, you can transfer the mixture, in batches, to a blender to puree, then return it to the slow cooker.

Plug in the slow cooker. Stir in the half-and-half or heavy cream, Parmesan cheese and tortellini. Cover and cook on high for an additional 15 to 30 minutes, until the tortellini is warmed through and tender. Stir in the fresh basil just before serving with plenty of additional shredded Parmesan on the side.

HEARTY TEX-MEX CHICKEN CHILI

Chili is a popular choice in our house, and since it's so easy to prepare and there are so many variations, I include it on the menu at least a couple of times a month all through the year. We're crazy for Tex-Mex flavors, and this chili delivers in a big way. It's rich, deliciously seasoned and loaded with chicken, red bell pepper, corn and two kinds of beans. You can let it simmer away on the stove for a couple of hours on a lazy Sunday afternoon or get it going in your slow cooker for an easy weeknight meal.

SERVES 8

3 tbsp (45 ml) vegetable oil, divided

2 lbs (910 g) boneless, skinless chicken breasts, cut into bite-size pieces

1 tsp salt, plus more to taste

1 tsp freshly ground black pepper, divided

1 cup (150 g) diced yellow onion

1 large red bell pepper, diced

1 jalapeño pepper, seeded and diced

2 tsp (6 g) minced garlic

1 (28-oz [800-g]) can crushed tomatoes

1 (14.5-oz [410-g]) can diced tomatoes, undrained

1 cup (240 ml) low-sodium chicken broth (I like Better Than Bouillon)

2 tbsp (18 g) chili powder

1 tsp ground cumin

1 tsp Mexican oregano

1 tsp ground coriander

1 (16-oz [455-g]) can kidney beans, rinsed and drained

1 (16-oz [455-g]) can cannellini (white kidney) beans, rinsed and drained

1½ cups (220 g) frozen corn kernels

¼ cup (10 g) chopped fresh cilantro, for serving

OPTIONAL TOPPINGS

Cheese, sour cream, avocado, cilantro, hot sauce

SLOW-COOKER METHOD

Pour 2 tablespoons (30 ml) of vegetable oil into the bottom of a large pot or Dutch oven and place it over medium heat. Add the chicken and cook about 5 to 6 minutes, stirring, until it is cooked through and the juices run clear. Season the chicken with the salt and ½ teaspoon of black pepper as it cooks. Transfer the chicken along with the cooking liquids from the pot to a 6-quart (5.5-L) slow cooker.

Add the remaining 1 tablespoon (15 ml) of oil to the pot, and add the onion, bell pepper and jalapeño pepper. Cook and stir until the onion and peppers just begin to soften, about 3 to 4 minutes. Add the garlic and cook and stir for 1 minute. Transfer the contents of the skillet to the slow cooker with the chicken.

Stir the crushed tomatoes, diced tomatoes and broth into the slow cooker with the chicken and season it with the chili powder, cumin, Mexican oregano, coriander and remaining ½ teaspoon of black pepper. Stir the mixture well, set the slow cooker to low and cook for 4 to 6 hours.

Remove the cover and stir in the kidney and cannellini beans and corn. Cover and cook for an additional 30 to 60 minutes. Sprinkle the cilantro over the top and serve with your choice of optional toppings.

ONE-POT METHOD

Pour 2 tablespoons (30 ml) of vegetable oil into the bottom of a large pot or Dutch oven and place it over medium heat. Add the chicken and cook, stirring, until the chicken until it is cooked through and the juices run clear, about 5 to 6 minutes. Season the chicken with the salt and ½ teaspoon of black pepper as it cooks. Transfer the chicken to a plate and set it aside.

Add the remaining 1 tablespoon (15 ml) of oil to the pot and add the onion, bell pepper and jalapeño pepper. Cook and stir until the onion and peppers just begin to soften, about 3 to 4 minutes. Add the garlic and cook and stir for 1 minute. Add the crushed tomatoes, diced tomatoes, broth and kidney and cannellini beans, and season with the chili powder, cumin, Mexican oregano, coriander and the remaining ½ teaspoon of black pepper. Return the cooked chicken to the pot and stir it well to combine.

Bring the mixture to a simmer over medium-high heat, then reduce the heat to low. Cover and simmer the chili for 2 hours, stirring occasionally. Remove the cover, stir in the corn and let the chili simmer for an additional 5 minutes. Sprinkle the cilantro over the top and serve with your choice of optional toppings.

(See photo on page 88)

BEEFY GAME-DAY BEER CHILI

When the party's at your house for the next big game, a slow cooker full of this chili is definitely in order. Rich, dark beer and mild poblano peppers add incredible flavor to this robust chili. While poblanos are typically roasted, sautéing them briefly before adding them to the slow cooker is also an excellent way to coax out their flavor. If your group is sensitive to heat, you can omit or reduce the amount of red pepper flakes. This recipe yields a substantial amount of chili, making it the perfect choice for your game-day crowd.

SERVES 8 TO 10

2 tbsp (30 ml) olive oil, divided

2½ lbs (1.2 kg) ground beef

1½ cups (105 g) diced white or yellow onion

2 medium poblano peppers, seeded and chopped

2 tsp (6 g) minced garlic

1 (28-oz [800-g]) can crushed tomatoes with added puree

2 (14.5-oz [410-g]) cans fire-roasted diced tomatoes, undrained

1 (11.2-oz [314-ml]) bottle dark beer (I like Guinness Stout)

1 (8-oz [170-g]) can tomato sauce

¼ cup (36 g) chili powder

2 tbsp (20 g) ground cumin

2 tbsp (4 g) dried oregano

2 tsp (6 g) ground coriander

½ tsp red pepper flakes, or to taste, optional

Freshly ground black pepper, to taste

1 (16-oz [455-g]) can kidney beans, rinsed and drained

1 (16-oz [455-g]) can pinto beans, rinsed and drained

OPTIONAL TOPPINGS

Sour cream, thinly sliced green onions, grated sharp cheddar cheese

In a large skillet, heat 1 tablespoon (15 ml) of olive oil over medium-high heat. Add the beef and cook for 5 to 6 minutes, stirring to crumble the meat, until no pink remains. Drain off as much of the grease as possible from the skillet and transfer the beef to the insert of a 6-quart (5.5-L) slow cooker.

Add the remaining 1 tablespoon (15 ml) of olive oil to the skillet and reduce the heat to medium. Add the onion and poblanos. Sauté for several minutes, then add the garlic and cook another 1 to 2 minutes, until the onion and peppers have softened.

Transfer the onion mixture to the slow cooker with the beef. Add the crushed tomatoes, diced tomatoes, beer, tomato sauce, chili powder, cumin, oregano, coriander, red pepper flakes (if using) and black pepper. Stir the mixture to combine it well. Cover and cook for 6 hours on low or for 3 hours on high. Add the rinsed and drained kidney and pinto beans, then cover and continue to cook for an additional 30 to 60 minutes.

Garnish individual servings with the optional toppings, as desired.

CHICKEN PARMESAN SOUP WITH CRUMBLED CROUTONS

When you need a quick, easy meal and don't want to deal with a pile of dishes, this soup fits the bill perfectly. It takes under 30 minutes to prepare, from start to finish, and it all takes place in one pot. Dry pasta is simmered right along with the other ingredients and cooks up perfectly al dente. Crumbled, store-bought croutons sprinkled on top add great flavor and texture and drive home the chicken Parmesan theme. This is a wonderful no-fuss, busy-day meal.

SERVES 6

2 tbsp (30 ml) olive oil

1½ lbs (675 g) boneless, skinless chicken breast, cut into bite-size pieces

½ cup (75 g) diced onion

½ tsp salt, plus more to taste

Freshly ground black pepper, to taste

2 tsp (6 g) minced garlic

3 tbsp (30 g) tomato paste

½ tsp red pepper flakes

1 (14.5-oz [410-g]) can fire-roasted diced tomatoes, undrained

6 cups (1.4 L) low-sodium chicken broth (I like Better Than Bouillon)

8 oz (225 g) dry short pasta (fusilli, penne and elbow macaroni all make good choices)

½ cup (90 g) finely grated Parmesan cheese, plus more for garnish

¼ cup (10 g) chopped fresh Italian parsley

1 cup (120 g) shredded mozzarella cheese

1 cup (30 g) cheese and garlic–flavored croutons, lightly crushed

Pour the olive oil into a large pot or Dutch oven and place it over medium heat. When the oil is hot, add the chicken and onion. Season the mixture with the salt and pepper, and sauté until the chicken is cooked through and the onion is tender, about 5 to 6 minutes. Add the garlic and cook for an additional 1 to 2 minutes, until fragrant. Add the tomato paste and red pepper flakes and stir to combine well. Add the diced tomatoes, broth and dry pasta. Bring the mixture to a boil over medium-high heat, then reduce the heat to low and simmer, covered, until the pasta is al dente, about 8 to 10 minutes.

Remove the pot from the heat, then stir in the Parmesan cheese and parsley and season with additional salt and pepper.

Garnish individual servings with the mozzarella cheese, crushed croutons and a little Parmesan cheese.

THREE-BEAN VEGGIE CHILI

Hearty and with tons of flavor, this bean- and veggie-loaded chili is a great way to go meatless. It's quick to prepare in one pot on the stove for a wholesome meal any time you're feeling the need to lighten things up. Color, texture and flavor are abundant in this tasty chili!

SERVES 6

2 tbsp (30 ml) olive oil

1 cup (150 g) diced onion

2 stalks celery, diced

1 medium carrot, peeled and diced

1 red bell pepper, seeded and diced

1 jalapeño, seeded and diced

2 tsp (6 g) minced garlic

2 tbsp (18 g) chili powder

2 tsp (6 g) ground cumin

1 tsp paprika

1 tsp dried oregano

½ tsp salt

½ tsp freshly ground black pepper

1 (28-oz [800-g]) can crushed tomatoes

1 (14.5-oz [410-g]) can diced tomatoes, undrained

2 cups (480 ml) vegetable broth

1 (16-oz [455-g]) can kidney beans, drained and rinsed

1 (16-oz [455-g]) can pinto beans, drained and rinsed

1 (16-oz [455-g]) can garbanzo beans, drained and rinsed

1 bay leaf

1½ cups (220 g) frozen corn

1 (6–7" [15–18-cm]) zucchini, chopped

OPTIONAL TOPPINGS

Cilantro, lime wedges, avocado, tortilla chips, sour cream, crumbled cotija cheese, cheddar cheese or Monterey Jack cheese

Warm the olive oil in a Dutch oven over medium heat. Add the onion, celery, carrot, bell pepper and jalapeño. Cook, stirring for 3 to 4 minutes, until the vegetables are tender. Add the garlic, chili powder, cumin, paprika, oregano, salt and black pepper. Cook and stir for 1 minute to lightly toast the spices. Add the crushed tomatoes, diced tomatoes, broth, the kidney, pinto and garbanzo beans and the bay leaf. Stir to combine the mixture, then increase the heat to medium-high and bring the mixture to a boil. Reduce the heat to low, cover the pot and simmer for at least 30 minutes and up to 1 hour.

Remove and discard the bay leaf and stir in the corn and zucchini. Simmer, uncovered, for 15 minutes, until the zucchini is fork-tender.

Ladle the chili into bowls and serve with the optional toppings, as desired.

BALSAMIC BEEF STEW

This soul-warming stew is both rustic and refined. Taking a few minutes to sear the beef and sauté the red onion, celery and garlic with a mixture of tomato paste, red wine and rosemary gives the stew a head start in the flavor department. A little balsamic vinegar is added toward the end of the cooking time to create this unique and truly delicious take on classic beef stew.

SERVES 4 TO 6

2 lbs (910 g) boneless beef chuck roast, trimmed and cut into bite-size pieces

1 tsp all-purpose seasoning (I like Lawry's Seasoned Salt)

Freshly ground black pepper, to taste

3 tbsp (45 ml) olive oil, divided

1 cup (150 g) diced red onion

½ cup (50 g) diced celery

2 tsp (6 g) minced garlic

2 tsp (2 g) dried crushed rosemary

2 tbsp (20 g) tomato paste

1 cup (240 ml) full-bodied red wine (like cabernet sauvignon, zinfandel, syrah or merlot)

2 cups (480 ml) low-sodium beef broth

1 lb (450 g) baby red and/or gold potatoes, halved or quartered

3 large carrots, peeled and cut into 1" (3-cm) chunks

2 bay leaves

3 tbsp (45 ml) water

3 tbsp (30 g) cornstarch

¼ cup (60 ml) balsamic vinegar

¼ cup (10 g) chopped fresh Italian parsley

Salt, to taste

Lay the pieces of chuck roast out on a large piece of foil, and season them with the all-purpose seasoning and black pepper, tossing to coat the pieces on all sides.

Heat 2 tablespoons (30 ml) of olive oil in a large heavy pot or Dutch oven over medium-high heat. Add the meat to the pot in a single layer, in batches if necessary to avoid overcrowding. Cook, turning as needed, until the meat is browned on all sides, about 6 to 8 minutes. Use a slotted spoon to transfer the meat to the slow cooker.

Add the remaining 1 tablespoon (15 ml) of olive oil to the beef drippings in the pot, then add the onion and celery. Sauté over medium heat until they are softened, about 2 to 3 minutes. Add the garlic and sauté for 1 minute. Season with the rosemary, and stir the tomato paste into the mixture. Add the wine and cook, stirring, for 1 to 2 minutes to bring the mixture to a simmer. Transfer the contents of the pot to the slow cooker with the beef. Add the broth, potatoes, carrots and bay leaves to the slow cooker and stir well to combine.

Cover and cook for 7 to 8 hours on low or for 3 to 4 hours on high, just until the beef and vegetables are fork-tender. About 30 minutes before the end of the cooking time, combine the water with the cornstarch in a small bowl. Stir the balsamic vinegar and the cornstarch slurry into the slow cooker. Cover and cook for the remaining 30 minutes, until the sauce is slightly thickened. Discard the bay leaves, stir in the parsley and season with salt and additional pepper before serving, if desired.

> **TIP:** Many grocery stores carry trimmed and cut chuck roast that is labeled "Beef for Stew." This is a great timesaver when prepping this recipe. Be sure to cut any large chunks in half so you have uniform, bite-size pieces.

30-MINUTE MINESTRONE

Colorful veggies are the basis for this classic and comforting minestrone soup. Get the most flavor and texture from your vegetables by simmering them for just long enough to cook the dry pasta until perfectly al dente. The entire recipe takes place in one pot on the stove, making it a no-sweat choice for busy days.

To make your meat lovers happy, add cooked, shredded chicken (like All-Purpose Chicken on page 41) or cooked and drained lean ground beef or turkey at the end of the cooking time.

SERVES 6 TO 8

2 tbsp (30 ml) olive oil

1 cup (150 g) diced white or yellow onion

1 cup (110 g) chopped carrots

3 celery ribs, chopped

1 cup (150 g) chopped zucchini

2 tsp (6 g) minced garlic

6 cups (1.4 L) low-sodium chicken or vegetable broth

1 (16-oz [455-g]) can cannellini beans, rinsed and drained

1 (16-oz [455-g]) can kidney beans, rinsed and drained

1 (28-oz [800-g]) can Italian-style crushed tomatoes

2 tsp (2 g) Italian seasoning

½ tsp salt, or to taste

Freshly ground black pepper, to taste

1 cup (100 g) dry ditalini or small elbow pasta

1 cup (145 g) frozen green beans

½ cup (20 g) chopped fresh Italian parsley

Shredded Parmesan cheese, for serving, optional

Heat the oil in a Dutch oven and add the onion, carrots, celery and zucchini. Cook, stirring occasionally, for 5 to 6 minutes, just until slightly softened. Add the garlic and sauté for an additional 2 to 3 minutes.

Add the broth, cannellini and kidney beans, tomatoes, Italian seasoning, salt and pepper. Bring the mixture to a boil, and add the pasta and green beans. Stir to combine, return the mixture to a boil, then reduce the heat to low. Cover and cook for 10 to 15 minutes, until the pasta is al dente. Stir in the parsley. Simmer for 2 minutes, then remove the pot from the heat.

Ladle the soup into bowls and sprinkle it with shredded Parmesan cheese, if desired.

Stored in an airtight container, this soup will keep well refrigerated for several days or frozen for 2 to 3 months. Soups containing pasta will thicken quite a bit when refrigerated, so add additional broth when reheating, as needed.

PULLED PORK CHILI

We do chili so often in this house that I've spent a lot of time in my kitchen experimenting with different cuts of meat, beans and spices to keep it interesting. This Pulled Pork Chili is one of our favorites. After cooking low and slow for a good part of the day, the lean pork shreds into a deliciously seasoned sauce. Corn and two kinds of beans are added toward the end of the cooking time to create even more flavor, color contrast and texture.

Serve this chili with tortilla chips or slices of cornbread warm from the oven for a hearty, satisfying meal.

SERVES 6 TO 8

2–2¼ lbs (900 g–1 kg) boneless pork loin or tenderloin, cut into 3–4" (8–10-cm) chunks

1 tsp salt

Freshly ground black pepper

2 tbsp (30 ml) olive oil

1 cup (150 g) diced yellow onion

1 jalapeño, seeded and diced

1 tsp minced garlic

1 (28-oz [800-g]) can crushed tomatoes

1 (14.5-oz [410-g]) can diced tomatoes, undrained

1 (4-oz [115-g]) can diced green chiles, drained

1 cup (240 ml) low-sodium beef broth

2 tbsp (18 g) chili powder

2 tsp (6 g) cumin

1 tsp oregano

1 tsp smoked paprika

1 (16-oz [450-g]) can chili beans in sauce, undrained

1 (16-oz [450-g]) can pinto beans, rinsed and drained

1 cup (145 g) frozen corn

Tortilla chips and/or cornbread, for serving

OPTIONAL TOPPINGS

Cilantro, thinly sliced green onions, avocado, sour cream, hot sauce

Season the pork with the salt and pepper.

Place a large skillet over medium heat and add the olive oil. Add the pork and sear for 2 to 3 minutes on each side, then transfer the pork to a 6-quart (5.5-L) slow cooker. Add the onion, jalapeño and garlic to the skillet, and sauté until the onion is translucent, about 3 or 4 minutes. Transfer the mixture from the skillet to the slow cooker with the pork.

Add the crushed tomatoes, diced tomatoes, chiles, broth, chili powder, cumin, oregano, paprika and pepper to taste. Cover and cook for 7 to 8 hours on low or 3½ to 4 hours on high, until the pork is tender and easy to shred.

Use two forks to shred the pork into the sauce in the slow cooker. Add the chili and pinto beans and corn, cover and continue to cook for an additional 30 to 60 minutes on low.

Ladle the chili into bowls and serve with the tortilla chips and/or cornbread and optional toppings, as desired.

ON THE SIDE

This chapter covers a wide range of side-dish options that will work for everything from simple weeknight dinners to summer barbecues and holiday gatherings.

Whatever the occasion, using your slow cooker to create recipes like Sweet Potatoes with Brown Sugar–Cinnamon Pecans (page 113) or Loaded Twice-Cooked Potatoes (page 118) is a great way to make enough to feed your group without hogging your big casserole dishes, pots and valuable oven space.

The Peach Applesauce (page 126) is a standout favorite in my house. It is a fantastic weekend meal prep option that can be frozen, if desired, but we never have a problem going through a batch in just a few days.

In addition to these slow-cooker choices, you'll find three wonderful one-pot side dishes, including the quickest and easiest method for creating perfectly tender yeast rolls (page 117) that may forever change your mind about baking rolls from scratch.

SWEET POTATOES WITH BROWN SUGAR–CINNAMON PECANS

I serve mashed sweet potatoes all year long as a side dish for everything from fish to chicken to steak, but this version with sweet, cinnamon-spiced pecans is especially well-suited for your holiday table. There's no good reason to waste valuable stove and oven space on recipes that can be done just as well in your slow cooker. Prepare the pecans in advance for a hassle-free addition to your holiday menu.

SERVES 8 TO 10

4 lbs (1.8 kg) red-skinned sweet potatoes, peeled and cut into 2" (5-cm) chunks

2 cups (480 ml) water

½ cup (120 g) sour cream

2 tbsp (28 g) butter, cut into small pieces

¼ cup (55 g) packed light brown sugar

1 tsp cinnamon

¼ tsp nutmeg

¼ tsp salt, or to taste

¼ cup (60 ml) milk, or as needed to reach desired consistency

BROWN SUGAR–CINNAMON PECANS

1 tbsp (14 g) butter

1 tbsp (9 g) light brown sugar

½ tsp cinnamon

Dash of salt

½ cup (60 g) chopped pecans

Place the chunks of sweet potato and the water in the insert of a 6-quart (5.5-L) slow cooker. Cover and cook for 5 to 6 hours on low or 3 to 4 hours on high, until the sweet potatoes are tender when pierced with the tip of a sharp knife. Use a slotted spoon to transfer the sweet potatoes to a large bowl.

Using oven mitts, lift the slow-cooker insert out of the base and discard the cooking liquid. Return the slow-cooker insert to the base and transfer the sweet potatoes back to the empty but still-warm slow-cooker insert.

Power off and unplug the slow cooker. Add the sour cream, butter, brown sugar, cinnamon, nutmeg and salt. Use an electric hand mixer to combine well. Add the milk, and mix until creamy. Transfer the mixture to a serving dish, or if you prefer, you can serve them straight from the slow cooker.

Prepare the pecans at least 30 minutes before the end of the cooking time. They can be prepared up to 24 hours in advance and stored in an airtight container.

To prepare them, melt the butter in a small skillet over medium-low heat. Add the brown sugar, cinnamon and salt, and stir for 1 minute to combine and to allow the sugar to begin to dissolve. Add the pecans and toss them with the mixture. Continue to cook and stir for 2 to 3 minutes to lightly toast the pecans.

Pour the mixture onto a sheet of wax or parchment paper, and spread it out in an even layer. Allow it to cool for about 20 to 30 minutes.

Sprinkle the Brown Sugar–Cinnamon Pecans over the sweet potatoes and serve immediately.

CHEESY CAULIFLOWER MASHED POTATOES

Cauliflower is a miracle vegetable, plain and simple. It's delicious on its own but can also stand in for so many other things, from pizza crust to tater tots and, in this recipe, cheesy mashed potatoes. And it really does do it miraculously. This cauliflower-potato combo is a delicious and familiar way to introduce cauliflower to your little ones. If it seems like there is too much liquid at the end of the cooking process, don't be concerned. After mashing the potatoes and cauliflower with the other ingredients, much of the liquid will be absorbed to achieve a perfectly creamy result.

SERVES 6

1 good-size head of cauliflower (approximately 2½ lbs [1.2 kg])

2 lbs (910 g) Yukon Gold potatoes, peeled and chopped into 2" (5-cm) chunks

1 tsp minced garlic

1 cup (240 ml) low-sodium chicken or vegetable broth

¼ cup (55 g) butter, cut into pats

½ tsp salt, plus more to taste

Freshly ground black pepper, to taste

½ cup (120 ml) sour cream

2 oz (60 g) cream cheese, softened

1 cup (120 g) shredded sharp cheddar cheese

¼ cup (45 g) grated Parmesan cheese

1 tbsp (3 g) fresh Italian parsley, for garnish

Trim the cauliflower head from the stem and chop it into small florets. Rinse with cold water and drain well. Transfer the cauliflower and the potatoes to a 6-quart (5.5-L) slow cooker.

Add the garlic, broth, butter, salt and pepper. Cover and cook for 4 hours on high, until tender.

Add the sour cream and cream cheese. Use a potato masher to coarsely mash the mixture. I think these are best with a little texture, so avoid overmashing. Use a spoon to stir in the cheddar and Parmesan cheeses. Season with additional salt and black pepper, if desired. Garnish with parsley and serve.

PERFECTLY TENDER SKILLET DINNER ROLLS

Is there anything more satisfying than producing a warm batch of fresh, homemade yeast rolls? These turn an otherwise average dinner into something really special.

YIELDS 12 ROLLS

1¾–2¼ cups (220–280 g) all-purpose flour, divided (see Note)

1 (0.25-oz [7-g]) envelope rapid-rise yeast

6 tbsp (90 g) softened butter, divided

¼ cup (50 g) granulated sugar

½ tsp salt

¾ cup (180 ml) milk

1 egg

NOTE: Do not add all of the flour at the beginning. Instead, add it in increments and judge as you go. You may not need the entire amount. And remember: a soft dough will result in tender rolls, which is exactly what we want!

Combine 1 cup (125 g) of flour, the yeast, 3 tablespoons (45 g) of softened butter, the sugar and the salt in the bowl of a stand mixer with the paddle attachment in place. Mix for 2 to 3 minutes to combine the ingredients.

Warm the milk for about 30 seconds in the microwave. The temperature should measure between 120 and 130°F (55°C) on an instant-read thermometer (this is vital to activating the yeast properly). Add the warmed milk to the flour mixture, and beat for about 1 minute, until well combined. Add the egg and beat on medium speed for another 1 to 2 minutes. Add ½ cup (65 g) of flour and beat for 2 minutes on medium speed. Stir in only as much of the remaining ¼ to ¾ cup (30 to 95 g) of flour as needed, in small increments, to make a soft, sticky dough. You may not need to use the entire amount of flour. When the dough is just beginning to hold together in a ball but is still very sticky, coat your hands with some flour and gather the dough up, scraping off the sticky dough from the bottom and sides of the bowl. Use your hands to form it into a neat ball. Set the dough down onto a floured board, cover it with a clean kitchen towel and let it rest.

Meanwhile, melt 1 tablespoon (14 g) of butter in a 10-inch (25-cm) cast-iron or other heavy, ovenproof skillet over low heat. Swirl the pan to coat it with the butter and remove it from the heat.

Divide the dough into 12 equal pieces and shape them into smooth balls. Place them in a circular pattern in the still-slightly-warm, greased skillet, leaving a little space between each ball. Cover the skillet with a clean kitchen towel, and let the dough rise in a warm, draft-free place until the rolls are nearly double in size, about 30 to 45 minutes.

While the dough is rising, preheat your oven to 375°F (190°C).

Transfer the skillet to the preheated oven and bake for 10 minutes. Melt the remaining 2 tablespoons (28 g) of butter, and brush about half of it over the rolls. Bake the rolls for an additional 5 to 10 minutes, until lightly browned. Remove the pan from the oven and immediately brush the rolls with any remaining butter.

I love to serve these rolls warm from the oven with all of the soups and stews included in this book or slathered with butter and jam for breakfast.

LOADED TWICE-COOKED POTATOES

If you love twice-baked potatoes (and who doesn't?) this recipe is going to make you very happy. Red-skinned potatoes are cooked until perfectly tender, then mashed right in the slow cooker with a delicious list of ingredients. This luscious mashed-potato casserole is easy to customize with a variety of different cheeses. For a little kick, add some pepper Jack, or for a creamy, smooth flavor, go with Gouda. Cooking the potatoes with the skin on adds color and texture to this dish and really drives home the flavor of a twice-baked potato, skin and all.

SERVES 6 TO 8

3 lbs (1.3 kg) red potatoes, unpeeled

1½ cups (360 ml) low-sodium chicken broth (I like Better Than Bouillon)

¾ cup (180 ml) milk, warmed for 30 seconds in the microwave

2 tbsp (28 g) butter

1½ cups (180 g) shredded cheddar cheese

¾ cup (180 g) light or regular sour cream

5 slices of bacon, cooked and crumbled, divided

3 tbsp (9 g) chopped fresh chives, divided

½ tsp all-purpose seasoning (I like Lawry's Seasoned Salt), or to taste

Wash the unpeeled potatoes and cut them into large 2- to 3-inch (5- to 8-cm) chunks. Place them in a 6-quart (5.5-L) slow cooker and add the broth. Cover and cook for 3 to 4 hours on high, until the potatoes are very tender when pierced with the tip of a sharp knife.

Power off and unplug the slow cooker. Use an electric hand mixer or potato masher to lightly mash the potatoes into the broth in the slow cooker. Add the milk and butter, and mash again until mostly creamy. You can mash as much as you'd like, but I prefer to leave a little texture.

Use a wooden spoon to stir in the cheddar cheese, sour cream, most of the bacon and chives (reserve a little of both for garnishing) and the all-purpose seasoning. Taste and add additional seasoning, if desired. Cover and cook on high for an additional 30 minutes, until heated through.

If you'd like, you can transfer the mixture to a serving bowl and garnish it with the reserved bacon and chives, or garnish and serve them directly from the slow cooker.

GARLIC-HERB-BUTTER CORN ON THE COB

Corn on the cob is one of those things that can be tricky to time. Once my husband fires up the grill, we always seem to get gabbing, and my timing can be thrown way off. The slow cooker is far more forgiving than a boiling pot of water, so this method comes in handy for a relaxed summer meal, eliminating the need to keep an eye on the pot. I can fit six big ears of corn in my roomy six-quart (5.5-L) slow cooker. If you're having trouble making them fit, snap the ears of corn in half before wrapping them in the foil.

SERVES 6

6 tbsp (84 g) butter, softened

1 tbsp (3 g) chopped fresh Italian parsley

¾ tsp granulated garlic or garlic powder

½ tsp salt

6 ears of sweet corn, husks and silks removed

Combine the butter, parsley, granulated garlic and salt in a small bowl. Place an ear of sweet corn on a sheet of foil large enough to enclose it (approximately 12 × 12-inches [30 × 30-cm]) and spread it with 1 tablespoon (14 g) of the butter mixture. Wrap the ear of corn tightly in the foil, being sure that the ends are secure, and place it in a 6-quart (5.5-L) oval slow cooker. Repeat with the remaining corn and butter mixture.

Cover the slow cooker and cook the corn for 4 hours on low or for 2 to 2½ hours on high. If your slow cooker is full to the top, it may take longer to cook. Switch to the warm setting to keep the corn warm for up to 1 hour.

HONEY-ORANGE BUTTERED CARROTS

This simple vegetable side dish is easily made in your slow cooker. Spoon the buttery, honey-orange liquid from the slow cooker over the tender carrots after cooking, or take a few minutes to simmer it on the stove to create a more glaze-like consistency.

SERVES 6 TO 8

2 lbs (910 g) carrots, peeled and sliced slightly on the diagonal into 1½" (4-cm) pieces

¼ cup (55 g) butter, melted

¼ cup (60 ml) honey

1 tbsp (15 ml) fresh orange juice

1 tsp orange zest

½ tsp salt

2 tbsp (6 g) chopped fresh chives or fresh Italian parsley

Coat the insert of a 5- to 6-quart (4.7- to 5.5-L) slow cooker with nonstick cooking spray

Add the carrots to the prepared slow cooker. Combine the butter, honey, orange juice, orange zest and salt in a small bowl. Pour the mixture over the carrots and toss to coat. Cover and cook on low for 5 to 6 hours or on high for 3 hours, until the carrots are fork-tender.

Use a slotted spoon to transfer the carrots to a serving dish, and spoon the liquid from the slow cooker over the top. Or, if you'd like to thicken the sauce to more of a glaze consistency, transfer the sauce to a small saucepan and bring it to a low boil over medium-high heat. Reduce the heat to medium and simmer it for 2 to 3 minutes, until it reaches a syrupy consistency. Drizzle the glaze over the carrots, toss to combine and sprinkle on the chives or parsley.

BACKYARD BARBECUE BAKED BEANS

No summer barbecue menu is complete without a big pot of baked beans. This substantial version includes ground beef, onion, bell pepper, a trio of canned beans and your favorite barbecue sauce. The one-pot method takes it from the stovetop to the oven to cook to bubbly perfection. These beefy, flavorful beans are a family favorite.

SERVES 8 TO 10

5 slices of bacon

1 lb (450 g) lean ground beef

1 cup (150 g) chopped onion

1 cup (110 g) chopped green bell pepper

1 tsp minced garlic

1 (28-oz [800-g]) can pork and beans, drained

1 (28-oz [800-g]) can pork and beans, with liquid

1 (16-oz [455-g]) can kidney beans, drained

1 (16-oz [455-g]) can pinto beans, drained

1 cup (240 ml) barbecue sauce (I like Kinder's Mild BBQ Sauce)

½ cup (120 ml) ketchup

¼ cup (55 g) packed light brown sugar

1 tbsp (15 ml) cider vinegar

1 tsp salt

½ tsp ground black pepper

½ tsp smoked paprika

ONE-POT METHOD

Preheat the oven to 350°F (175°C).

Place the bacon in a large Dutch oven. Cook for about 3 to 4 minutes over medium-high heat until it's evenly browned. Transfer the bacon to paper towels to drain.

Drain the bacon grease from the pot, leaving just a scant amount. Reduce heat to medium. Place the ground beef, onion, bell pepper and garlic in the Dutch oven. Cook for 5 to 6 minutes, stirring to break up the beef, until it is completely browned and the onion and bell pepper are tender. Drain the excess grease from the pot.

Mix in the pork and beans, kidney beans, pinto beans, barbecue sauce, ketchup, brown sugar, vinegar, salt, black pepper and paprika. Stir to combine the mixture well. Crumble the bacon into the pot, and stir again to combine. Cover the Dutch oven and transfer it to the preheated oven. Bake the beans for 1 hour, until bubbly.

SLOW-COOKER METHOD

Prepare the beans as directed for the one-pot method, but instead of baking, transfer the mixture to a 6-quart (5.5-L) slow cooker and cook for 2 to 3 hours on low. Avoid cooking canned beans in a slow cooker for longer than 3 hours to keep them from becoming mushy and undesirable.

Transfer any leftovers to an airtight container and refrigerate for up to 3 to 4 days. The beans may be frozen in a freezer-safe container for up to 3 months.

PEACH APPLESAUCE

Silky, flavorful, made-from-scratch applesauce is a real treat, and the store-bought variety doesn't even compare. While homemade applesauce can be made year-round, I just love cooking up a batch in the fall months when apples are at their peak. The addition of frozen peaches adds a more complex summer fruit flavor any time of year. Use a combination of crisp, sweet apples like Gala, Fuji, Honeycrisp and creamy McIntosh apples for the best flavor and consistency. Since all apple varieties vary in sweetness, I add the honey as the last step so that the amount can be adjusted to taste. If your apples are sweet enough, you'll want to add only a touch of honey or possibly none at all. Pure vanilla extract and a touch of ground ginger add a little something extra to the flavor while still keeping it super kid-friendly.

YIELDS APPROXIMATELY 3 PINTS (1.4 L)

3 lbs (1.3 kg) assorted apples (Gala, Fuji, Honeycrisp and McIntosh), peeled, cored and cut into wedges

1 (16-oz [450-g]) bag frozen sliced peaches, thawed

¼ cup (60 ml) water

2 tbsp (30 ml) fresh lemon juice

1 tsp pure vanilla extract

½ tsp ground ginger

2 tbsp (30 ml) honey, or to taste

Place the apples and peaches in a 6-quart (5.5-L) slow cooker. Pour in the water, lemon juice, vanilla and ginger, and stir to combine. Cook for 3 hours on high or 5 hours on low.

Power off and unplug the slow cooker. Uncover, and with a potato masher, mash the applesauce until you get the consistency you want. If you like your applesauce smoother and less chunky, you can use an immersion blender to blend it as smooth as you like. Taste and add the honey to sweeten as needed. Let the applesauce cool for 30 minutes before refrigerating it.

This sauce can be stored in an airtight container in your refrigerator for up to 1 week, or transfer it to mason jars or other freezer-safe containers and freeze it for up to 8 months.

VEGETABLE RICE PILAF

A simple rice pilaf has always been one of my favorite side dishes. I like to use a combination of rice and orzo to start and then add in other easy-to-stock ingredients, like the frozen mixed veggies in this recipe. This is a side dish that can be thrown together on a whim in one pot on the stove in under 30 minutes. It is also a great way to add color to your plate and incorporate more veggies into a meal.

SERVES 4 TO 6

2 tbsp (28 g) butter

1 cup (110 g) uncooked long-grain white rice

½ cup (55 g) orzo

3 cups (720 ml) low-sodium chicken broth (I like Better Than Bouillon)

½ tsp salt

½ tsp garlic powder

¼ tsp onion powder

Freshly ground black pepper, to taste

1 cup (180 g) frozen mixed vegetables (I like to use a mix of green beans, corn, peas and carrots)

2 tbsp (6 g) chopped fresh Italian parsley

Melt the butter in a 12-inch (30-cm) skillet or sauté pan with a lid over medium heat. When the butter has melted, add the rice and orzo, and cook, stirring, for 3 to 4 minutes, until they are lightly toasted.

Carefully pour in the broth. Add the salt, garlic powder, onion powder and pepper. Stir to combine the mixture, and bring it to a low boil. Reduce the heat to low, cover the skillet and cook for 10 minutes. Remove the cover and add the frozen mixed vegetables. Cover and continue to cook for an additional 10 minutes, until the broth has been absorbed, the rice and orzo are tender and fluffy and the frozen vegetables are warmed through. Remove the skillet from the heat and stir in the parsley before serving.

TIP: To reheat leftovers, add a splash of water and microwave for 1 minute, until warmed through.

APPETIZERS AND SNACKS

If you think your slow cooker is good only for main dishes, think again! You can use it to create a variety of appetizers and snacks your family will love. This chapter includes wonderfully crunchy, munchy nibbles like the Honey Barbecue Snack Mix (page 138) and the Sweet Spiced Cocktail Nuts (page 137) that are perfect for movie nights, after school or snacks on the go.

And when putting together a party menu, your slow cooker should definitely be part of that plan! Get one of the appetizer recipes in this chapter started before party time, and there will be something warm for your guests to munch on as soon as they arrive. Warm, cheesy dips are always a popular choice, and I've included three of my favorites in this chapter—Meaty Queso Dip (page 141), Buffalo Chicken Dip (page 145) and Warm, Cheesy Crab-Artichoke Dip (page 142). All of these dips make for excellent party fare, and two include alternative directions for quickly and easily preparing them in a skillet. For more substantial choices, look to the Asian Sesame Party Meatballs (page 133) and the Sweet and Spicy Pineapple Barbecue Cocktail Sausage (page 134). These meaty choices are a great way to supplement a menu for a big group.

ASIAN SESAME PARTY MEATBALLS

There's something about the addition of sesame oil to a dish that makes it completely irresistible, and this recipe is no exception. That amazing toasted sesame flavor is excellent combined with fresh ginger and garlic in these tasty meatballs. After simmering in your slow cooker in a hoisin- and soy sauce–based sauce that's sweetened with brown sugar, they become one of the most fabulous party snacks ever! Have a large group coming? Double the recipe in a six-quart (5.7-L) slow cooker.

As much as I love serving these meatballs at parties, they also make for a simple dinner when served over rice with steamed broccoli or green beans.

SERVES 8

MEATBALLS

1 lb (450 g) lean ground pork

1 lb (450 g) lean ground beef

2 eggs

½ cup (20 g) panko bread crumbs

⅓ cup (66 g) grated onion

2 tsp (10 ml) toasted sesame oil

1 heaping tsp finely grated ginger root

1 tsp minced garlic

½ tsp salt

½ tsp freshly ground black pepper

SAUCE

½ cup (120 ml) hoisin sauce

½ cup (120 ml) light soy sauce

½ cup (120 ml) ketchup

⅓ cup (75 g) brown sugar

¼ cup (60 ml) dry sherry

2 tsp (10 g) finely grated ginger root

2 tsp (10 ml) sriracha, or to taste

1 tsp minced garlic

GARNISH

2 tbsp (30 g) sesame seeds

2 green onions, thinly sliced

Preheat the oven to 450°F (230°C). Line a large rimmed baking sheet with aluminum foil, and coat the foil with nonstick cooking spray.

In a large bowl, mix together the pork, beef, eggs, bread crumbs, onion, sesame oil, ginger, garlic, salt and pepper. Shape the mixture into 1½-inch (4-cm) diameter meatballs, and place them on the prepared baking sheet. You should end up with 26 to 28 meatballs. Bake the meatballs for 15 to 18 minutes, until lightly browned. They don't need to be completely cooked through at this point.

Meanwhile, coat the insert of a 4-quart (3.8-L) slow cooker with nonstick cooking spray. Combine the hoisin sauce, soy sauce, ketchup, brown sugar, sherry, ginger, sriracha and garlic in a small mixing bowl. Set aside the mixture.

Add the browned meatballs to the prepared slow cooker and pour the sauce over the top. Lightly toss the meatballs with a spoon to coat them with the sauce. Cover and cook on low for 2 hours, until the meatballs are cooked through and the sauce is bubbly.

Garnish with the sesame seeds and green onions and serve directly from the slow cooker, or transfer the meatballs to a platter to garnish and serve.

> NOTE: The sauce has just a touch of heat if you use the amount of sriracha indicated. Use less for a milder result, or more to kick it up!

SWEET AND SPICY PINEAPPLE BARBECUE COCKTAIL SAUSAGE

I love to include a fun, vintage appetizer like these glazed cocktail sausages on my party menus. This one has a bit of an unexpected but seriously delicious sweet, hot, tropical barbecue flavor that I feel confident your party guests will wholeheartedly embrace. They are perfect for a game day party, summer barbecue, New Year's Eve or anytime the craving strikes!

SERVES 12

2 (12-oz [340-g]) packages fully-cooked cocktail sausages (I like Lit'l Smokies® Smoked Sausage)

1 (8-oz [230-g]) can crushed pineapple in pineapple juice (not heavy syrup)

1 (11-oz [310-g]) jar red pepper jelly

½ cup (120 ml) barbecue sauce

¼ cup (55 g) light brown sugar

1 tbsp (10 g) cornstarch

Open the packages of sausages and drain and discard the excess liquid. Place the sausages in a 3- to 4-quart (2.8- to 3.8-L) slow cooker. Open the can of pineapple and drain and reserve the juice from the can for later.

Add the red pepper jelly, barbecue sauce, light brown sugar and the drained pineapple to a medium mixing bowl and stir until well combined. Pour the mixture into the slow cooker, and stir to combine it with the sausage. Cover and cook on low for 2 to 3 hours.

After the initial cooking time, combine 2 tablespoons (30 ml) of the reserved pineapple juice and the cornstarch in a small bowl, and stir the slurry into the sausage mixture. Cover and cook on high for an additional 30 minutes, until the sauce has thickened slightly.

Serve immediately, or switch the slow cooker to the warm setting to keep the sausage warm for up to 1 hour.

SWEET SPICED COCKTAIL NUTS

I was skeptical about roasting nuts in the slow cooker instead of the oven, but now that I've tried, it is doubtful my cocktail nuts will ever see the inside of an oven again. The slow cooker allows the nuts to retain some of their moisture, but they still roast up beautifully and crisp up as they cool.

Nuts are a wholesome snack and also make excellent gifts. Package them in mason jars to give to friends, family and coworkers at the holidays, and they'll be hooked! These roasted, toasted nuts are also wonderful chopped and added to a big green salad with a little crumbled blue cheese.

YIELDS 5 CUPS (600 G)

1 egg white

1 tbsp (15 ml) water

2 tsp (10 ml) pure vanilla extract

1 cup (120 g) roasted, salted almonds

1 cup (120 g) roasted, salted cashews

1 cup (120 g) roasted, salted peanuts

1 cup (120 g) pecan halves

1 cup (120 g) shelled walnuts

2 tsp (10 g) butter, melted and slightly cooled

½ cup (110 g) packed light brown sugar

1 tsp ground cinnamon

½ tsp ground ginger

¼ tsp ground nutmeg

¼ tsp ground cloves

⅛ tsp cayenne pepper, or to taste

Coat the insert of a 6-quart (5.5-L) slow cooker with nonstick cooking spray.

In a large bowl, whisk the egg white, water and vanilla until frothy, then stir in the almonds, cashews, peanuts, pecans and walnuts. Add the melted, slightly cooled butter and toss until the nuts are well coated. Transfer the nuts to the prepared slow cooker.

In a small bowl, combine the brown sugar, cinnamon, ginger, nutmeg, cloves and cayenne pepper. Sprinkle the mixture over the nuts in the slow cooker, and toss it all together.

Cover and cook on low for 3 hours. About half way through the cooking time, carefully remove the lid and stir the nuts. Wipe down the interior of the lid with a kitchen towel to dry it, then replace the cover and continue to cook for the remaining time.

Turn the nuts out onto a wax paper–lined baking sheet, and spread them out in an even layer. Let them cool completely. The nuts will crisp up as they cool.

Store them in airtight containers. They are best if consumed within 2 weeks.

HONEY BARBECUE SNACK MIX

This recipe takes me back to warm summer nights when the boys were young. They loved cereal snack mixes, and I frequently mixed up a big batch to take with us to the Fourth of July fireworks celebration. It's a great portable snack, but I also love to set out a bowlful on movie night. This version is sweet and savory, salty and crunchy and totally irresistible.

To ensure a good result, you'll need to use an oval 6-quart (5.5-L) or larger slow cooker so there's more space for the ingredients to spread out. The slow cooker does a great job of cooking up a big batch all at once, but this is not a set-it-and-forget-it recipe. It takes some babysitting but will free up oven space and keep the kitchen cool in the hot summer months.

YIELDS APPROXIMATELY 4 QUARTS (400 G)

3 cups (75 g) Corn Chex®

3 cups (75 g) Rice Chex®

2 cups (50 g) Cheerios®

2 cups (50 g) mini pretzels

1½ cups (180 g) honey-roasted peanuts

6 tbsp (84 g) butter, melted

⅓ cup (80 ml) vegetable oil

¼ cup (60 ml) honey

2 tbsp (20 g) Best-Ever Barbecue Seasoning Mix (page 185)

1 tbsp (15 ml) Worcestershire sauce

1 cup (25 g) cheese crackers, optional

Coat the insert of a 6-quart (5.5-L) or larger oval slow cooker with nonstick cooking spray. Add the Corn Chex, Rice Chex, Cheerios, pretzels and peanuts to the slow cooker, and toss them with a wooden spoon, being careful not to crush the ingredients.

In a small bowl, stir together the butter, vegetable oil, honey, Best-Ever Barbecue Seasoning Mix and Worcestershire sauce. Pour half of the mixture over the party mix, and toss it lightly. Add the remaining seasoned butter mixture, and toss again until the party mix is well coated.

Cover and cook on low for 2 hours, stirring from the bottom every 20 minutes during the cooking time. Every time you lift the cover, be sure to wipe down any condensation on the inside with a kitchen towel before placing it back on the slow cooker. Watch closely, and turn the slow cooker off once the mixture is beginning to get golden brown.

Turn the mixture out onto a large sheet of foil, and toss it lightly with the cheese crackers, if using. Allow it to cool slightly before serving.

This snack mix is delicious served warm or completely cooled. Once the mix has completely cooled, it can be transferred to airtight containers and stored for up to 1 week.

MEATY QUESO DIP

This irresistible cheesy dip is one of those no-sweat, easy-peasy recipes that will make you wonder why you ever work so hard on a party appetizer menu. After just a few minutes of prep, you toss all the ingredients into the slow cooker and come back to give it a stir every now and then as your guests arrive. This queso is at the top of the list of game-day favorites in my house.

Cheesy dips like this one are a great choice for the slow cooker. Ladle out just enough to fill a serving dish, and keep the rest in the slow cooker to stay warm and delicious for 1 to 2 hours. If you happen to have leftovers, store them in an airtight container in the refrigerator to reheat in the microwave the next day.

SERVES 12

½ lb (225 g) mild or spicy pork sausage (I like Jimmy Dean®)

1 cup (150 g) diced yellow onion

1 large jalapeño, seeded and diced

2 tbsp (18 g) Flavor Fiesta Taco Seasoning Mix (page 184) or store-bought taco seasoning

16 oz (450 g) Velveeta cheese, cut into cubes

8 oz (225 g) shredded sharp cheddar cheese

8 oz (225 g) shredded Monterey Jack cheese

2 (10-oz [280-g]) cans diced tomatoes and green chiles, undrained (I like RO*TEL®)

Tortilla chips, for serving

Place a 12-inch (30-cm) skillet over medium heat and add the sausage and onion. Cook for 4 to 5 minutes, stirring to break up the sausage, until the sausage is thoroughly cooked. Drain and discard the grease from the skillet. Return the skillet to the heat and add the jalapeño and Flavor Fiesta Taco Seasoning Mix. Cook and stir for another 1 to 2 minutes to lightly toast the spices.

Transfer the sausage mixture to a 6-quart (5.5-L) slow cooker. Add the Velveeta, cheddar cheese, Monterey Jack cheese and the tomatoes and green chiles. Stir well, cover and cook for 1½ to 2 hours on low, until the cheese is melted and smooth, stirring once about every 20 to 30 minutes during the cooking time.

Set the slow cooker to the warm setting. Transfer some of the queso to a serving bowl to set out with tortilla chips, and keep the rest in the slow cooker to stay warm for 1 to 2 hours, stirring every now and then to prevent it from burning.

WARM, CHEESY CRAB-ARTICHOKE DIP

I've been making different versions of creamy, cheesy dips for ages, and they just never go out of style. Here I've combined two of our favorites: warm crab dip and artichoke dip. Diced jarred jalapeños along with a little of the briny liquid from the jar add a tangy zip and just a touch of heat. I most frequently use the skillet method because it is so fast and easy, but it also works really well in the slow cooker if you'd like to prepare it and keep it warm. I like to serve this luscious dip with a lightly toasted, sliced baguette, but it is also wonderful next to a bowl of tortilla chips and a platter of fresh veggies.

SERVES 10

4 oz (115 g) regular or Neufchatel (reduced-fat) cream cheese

1½ cups (330 g) mayonnaise

1 cup (120 g) shredded mozzarella cheese, divided

½ cup (90 g) finely shredded Parmesan cheese, divided

1 (14-oz [400-g]) can artichoke hearts in water, drained and coarsely chopped

1 (8-oz [230-g]) can lump crab meat

10-15 jarred jalapeño slices, diced, with 2 tsp (10 ml) liquid reserved

½ tsp garlic powder

½ tsp all-purpose seasoning (I like Lawry's Seasoned Salt)

2 green onions, thinly sliced, for garnish, optional

1 French baguette, sliced, for serving

SLOW-COOKER METHOD

Coat the insert of a 2- to 4-quart (1.8- to 3.8-L) slow cooker with nonstick cooking spray.

Add the cream cheese, mayonnaise, mozzarella cheese, Parmesan cheese, artichokes, crab meat, jalapeños, reserved jalapeño liquid, garlic powder and all-purpose seasoning to the slow cooker. Mix to combine, then cover and cook on low for 2 hours, until the cream cheese has completely melted. Stir until completely smooth, then cover and cook for an additional 15 to 20 minutes, until bubbly. Garnish with green onions, if desired.

The dip will stay warm and creamy on the warm setting for up to 1 hour. Stir occasionally to prevent it from burning or separating.

ONE-POT METHOD

Preheat the oven to 400°F (200°C).

Add the cream cheese, mayonnaise, ¾ cup (90 g) of the mozzarella and ¼ cup (45 g) of the Parmesan cheeses to a 10-inch (25-cm) cast-iron skillet, and place over medium-low heat. Cook and stir until the mixture melts and is well combined. Remove it from the heat and stir in the artichokes, crab meat, jalapeños, reserved jalapeño liquid, garlic powder and all-purpose seasoning. Top with the remaining ¼ cup (30 g) of mozzarella and ¼ cup (45 g) of Parmesan.

Transfer the skillet to the preheated oven, and bake for about 15 minutes, until bubbly. Turn the oven to broil, and cook for an additional 2 or 3 minutes, until lightly golden brown. Remove the skillet from the oven, and sprinkle on the green onions, if desired.

SERVING

Preheat the oven to 400°F (200°C). Place the baguette slices in a single layer on a baking sheet and put them in the oven for about 5 minutes, until lightly toasted. Serve the dip alongside the lightly toasted baguette slices.

BUFFALO CHICKEN DIP

This outrageously addictive dip is guaranteed to be a hit with partygoers. My version of this party classic includes everything you love about buffalo chicken wings in a warm, mildly spicy dip. Everything takes place in your slow cooker or one 10-inch (25-cm) skillet, which makes it incredibly easy to put together for a sudden craving or last-minute gathering. The fast cleanup is a huge bonus.

The small amount of crumbled blue cheese is optional but highly recommended. It's just enough to drive home the buffalo-wing flavor without being overwhelming. I always serve this dip with Fritos corn chips, celery sticks and baby carrots, but tortilla chips and baguette slices are also great options.

SERVES 10

1 (8-oz [230-g]) package cream cheese, cut into 8 pieces

1 heaping cup (135 g) shredded mozzarella cheese

½ cup (120 ml) bottled ranch dressing

½ cup (120 ml) sour cream

½ cup (120 ml) buffalo wing sauce (I like Frank's RedHot® Buffalo Wings Sauce)

2 cups (250 g) chopped All-Purpose Chicken (page 41) or store-bought rotisserie chicken

2 tbsp (15 g) crumbled blue or Gorgonzola cheese

2 green onions, thinly sliced

DIPPERS

Celery sticks, baby carrots, sliced baguette, corn chips (like Fritos® Scoops!® Corn Chips) or tortilla chips

SLOW-COOKER METHOD
Coat a 2- to 4-quart (1.8- to 3.8-L) slow cooker insert with nonstick cooking spray. Add the cream cheese, mozzarella cheese, ranch dressing, sour cream, wing sauce, chicken and blue cheese. Stir to combine, then cover and cook on low for 2 hours, until the cream cheese has completely melted. Stir until completely smooth, then cover and cook for an additional 15 to 20 minutes, until bubbly.

Garnish the dip with the green onions, and serve it warm with celery sticks, baby carrots, baguette slices and corn chips for dipping.

The dip will stay warm and creamy on the warm setting for up to 1 hour. Stir occasionally to prevent it from burning or separating.

ONE-POT METHOD
Preheat the oven to 375°F (190°C).

Add the cream cheese and mozzarella cheese to a cast-iron 10-inch (25-cm) skillet or other heavy, ovenproof skillet, and place it over low heat. Cook for 4 to 5 minutes, stirring frequently, until the cheeses have melted. Remove the skillet from the heat, and stir in the ranch dressing, sour cream and wing sauce. Add the chicken and crumbled blue cheese, and stir until well combined.

Transfer the skillet to the oven, and bake for about 15 to 20 minutes, until bubbling.

Move the oven rack to about 6 inches (15 cm) from the heating element, and broil the dip until lightly browned. Remove the skillet from the oven, and let it stand for 5 minutes to cool slightly. The dip will seem a bit thin but will set up as it rests.

Garnish the dip with the green onions, and serve it warm with celery sticks, baby carrots, baguette slices and corn chips for dipping.

BREAKFAST AND BRUNCH

Whether you are hosting a holiday brunch, having a group over after church or looking for a quick and easy Sunday breakfast for your family, the recipes in this chapter have it covered.

The gentle low heat of the slow cooker does a fabulous job of preparing egg dishes like quiches, strata and layered breakfast casseroles. In this chapter you'll find several of these classic egg-based dishes that will serve a good-size group and will work perfectly for a late-morning brunch. But in my kitchen, these recipes are not limited to the morning hours. My boys are *big* on breakfast fare, so from the time they were very young, I've taken advantage of that fact and planned an easy breakfast-for-dinner menu at least once a month. The Sausage and Sweet Potato Breakfast Burrito Bowls (page 154) and the Bacon, Broccoli and Cheese Crustless Quiche (page 149) are both excellent choices any time of day or night.

For quick and easy breakfast options, look to the one-pot Roast Beef Hash and Eggs (page 162) or the Southwest Sausage–Tater Tot Breakfast Skillet (page 150). And for a sweet treat, your family will be very happy to wake up to the aroma of the heavenly Overnight Skillet Maple-Pecan Cinnamon Rolls (page 157) baking in the oven.

BACON, BROCCOLI AND CHEESE CRUSTLESS QUICHE

Quiche is a must on all of my brunch menus, and this heavenly slow-cooker version is a wonderful choice when serving a group. It's loaded with the family-friendly flavors of bacon, broccoli, Swiss cheese and sharp cheddar cheese. Serve it straight from the slow cooker for easy cleanup.

Don't be tempted to speed up the cooking time by setting your slow cooker on high. For slow-cooked egg dishes like quiches and strata, the low setting will turn out a light and fluffy texture. I prefer to use reduced-fat milk in this recipe, but feel free to substitute heavy cream or half-and-half for a richer result.

SERVES 8

2 tbsp (28 g) butter

1 cup (180 g) bite-size broccoli florets

½ cup (55 g) diced red bell pepper

½ cup (75 g) diced onion

½ tsp minced garlic

¾ tsp salt, divided

Freshly ground black pepper, to taste

1½ cups (180 g) shredded Swiss cheese

1 cup (120 g) shredded sharp cheddar cheese

12 large eggs

1½ cups (360 ml) milk

7 slices of bacon, cooked and crumbled

Coat the insert of a 6-quart (5.5-L) slow cooker with nonstick cooking spray.

Place the butter in a 12-inch (30-cm) skillet over medium heat. Add the broccoli, bell pepper, onion and garlic. Season with ¼ teaspoon of salt and a little black pepper. Cook, stirring occasionally, for 3 to 4 minutes, until the broccoli is bright green and just barely fork-tender. Transfer the cooked vegetables to the slow cooker, and spread them out in an even layer. Sprinkle the shredded Swiss and cheddar cheeses evenly over the vegetables.

Crack the eggs into a large mixing bowl, and whisk them vigorously with the milk, pepper and the remaining ½ teaspoon of salt. Pour the egg mixture over the vegetables and cheese, and sprinkle the cooked and crumbled bacon over the top. Cover and cook for 3 to 3½ hours on low, until a knife inserted in the center comes out clean.

TIP: For perfect crisp-cooked bacon, line a large rimmed baking sheet with aluminum foil, and place the bacon strips on the foil so that they aren't touching. Bake at 400°F (200°C) for 15 to 20 minutes, until cooked to the desired level of crispness. Remove the baking sheet from the oven and transfer the bacon to a double layer of paper towels to drain. Blot any excess grease with additional paper towels.

SOUTHWEST SAUSAGE–TATER TOT BREAKFAST SKILLET

When you think of breakfast potatoes, tater tots may not be the first thing that comes to mind, but they work so well in this easy breakfast skillet. I've added a Southwestern twist with colorful bell peppers and the cheesy goodness of shredded cheddar and pepper Jack cheeses. When this comes out of the oven, it's pretty much required that I set out sour cream and hot sauce for my group. Trust me on this: there's just something fun about eating tater tots for breakfast!

SERVES 6

2 tbsp (30 ml) olive oil, or as needed

8 oz (225 g) regular bulk pork sausage (I like Jimmy Dean's)

⅓ cup (35 g) diced red bell pepper

⅓ cup (35 g) diced green bell pepper

⅓ cup (50 g) diced onion

4 cups (450 g) frozen tater tots (about half of a 32-oz [910-g] bag)

¾ cup (90 g) shredded cheddar cheese

¾ cup (90 g) shredded pepper Jack cheese

10 large eggs

¾ cup (180 ml) milk

½ tsp salt

¼ tsp freshly ground black pepper

¼ tsp granulated garlic or garlic powder

¼ cup (12 g) thinly sliced green onions

FOR SERVING

Sour cream and hot sauce, optional

Preheat the oven to 350°F (175°C).

Pour the olive oil into a 12-inch (30-cm) cast-iron or other heavy, ovenproof skillet, and place it over medium heat. Add the sausage and cook for 4 to 5 minutes, stirring to break it up, until no pink remains. Remove the skillet from the heat, and use a slotted spoon to transfer the sausage to a plate lined with a double layer of paper towels to drain. Return the skillet to the heat, and add additional olive oil, if needed. Add the bell peppers and onion to the skillet, and sauté for 2 to 3 minutes, until softened. Remove the skillet from the heat, and transfer the bell peppers and onions to the plate with the sausage.

Pour the tater tots into the bottom of the empty skillet, and spread them out in an even layer. Scatter the sausage, peppers and onions over the top, and sprinkle with the cheddar and pepper Jack cheeses. Whisk the eggs, milk, salt, pepper and granulated garlic together in a medium mixing bowl, and pour the mixture over the top of the tater tots.

Transfer the skillet to the oven and bake for 30 to 35 minutes, until the egg mixture is set and the cheese has melted. Remove the skillet from the oven, and sprinkle it with the green onions. Let it rest for about 5 minutes before slicing and serving. We love this with a dollop of sour cream and hot sauce!

HASH BROWN BREAKFAST CASSEROLE

This substantial, layered breakfast casserole is loaded with hash browns, sausage, eggs and two kinds of cheese, and it is just the thing for when you've got a hungry group to feed. It's a great choice for everything from a holiday breakfast buffet to feeding your kid's swim team after an early morning swim meet. Top individual servings with sour cream and chives, and pass the hot sauce.

SERVES 10

1 lb (450 g) regular pork sausage

1 (20-oz [560-g]) package refrigerated shredded hash browns, divided

½ cup (75 g) diced onion, divided

½ cup (55 g) diced red bell pepper, divided

1 (4-oz [115-g]) can diced green chiles, drained, divided

1½ cups (180 g) shredded sharp cheddar cheese, divided

1 cup (120 g) shredded pepper Jack cheese, divided

12 large eggs

½ cup (120 ml) milk

½ tsp salt

½ tsp granulated garlic or garlic powder

¼ tsp dry ground mustard

¼ tsp freshly ground black pepper

OPTIONAL TOPPINGS

Sour cream, chives, hot sauce

Coat a 6-quart (5.5-L) slow cooker insert with nonstick cooking spray.

Place a 12-inch (30-cm) nonstick skillet over medium heat and add the sausage. Cook for 4 to 5 minutes, stirring to break it up, until browned and thoroughly cooked. Remove the skillet from the heat, and transfer the sausage to a double layer of paper towels to drain. Use additional paper towels to pat down the cooked sausage to remove as much of the excess grease as possible.

Layer half of the hash browns in the bottom of the slow cooker. Top with half the cooked sausage, onion, bell pepper, chiles, and cheddar and pepper Jack cheeses. Repeat to make another layer with the remaining half of the same ingredients.

Whisk together the eggs, milk, salt, granulated garlic, ground mustard and black pepper. Pour the egg mixture evenly over the top of the casserole. Cover and cook for 6 to 7 hours on low or 3 to 3½ hours on high, until the casserole is set up in the center and the edges are golden brown and beginning to pull away from the sides. Unplug the slow cooker, and using oven mitts, remove the insert from the base.

Let the casserole rest for 5 minutes, then slice and serve it with the optional toppings, if desired.

> **NOTE:** While slow-cooker egg dishes are usually best cooked on low, this more substantial casserole stands up well to higher temperatures. So feel free to cook on high if you need it in less time.

SAUSAGE AND SWEET POTATO BREAKFAST BURRITO BOWLS

My boys all love sweet potatoes, so I've pretty much prepared them every possible way and love to incorporate them into all kinds of recipes. Here they cook up perfectly tender in your slow cooker along with buttery Yukon Gold potatoes, pork sausage and pinto beans. Spoon the mixture into bowls for serving, add a fried or scrambled egg and let everyone add their toppings of choice.

In addition to being a unique and delicious choice for a late morning brunch, these hearty, flavorful burrito bowls make an excellent breakfast-for-dinner option.

SERVES 6

BURRITO BOWLS

1 lb (450 g) bulk ground pork sausage

1 large red-skinned sweet potato, peeled and chopped into 1" (3-cm) pieces

1 large Yukon Gold potato, peeled and chopped into 1" (3-cm) pieces

1 tbsp (9 g) Flavor Fiesta Taco Seasoning Mix (page 184) or store-bought taco seasoning

1 cup (240 ml) red salsa

½ cup (75 g) diced yellow onion

1 (4-oz [115-g]) can diced green chiles, drained

1 (16-oz [455-g]) can pinto beans

EGGS

¼ cup (55 g) butter, or as needed

6 large eggs

Salt and freshly ground black pepper, to taste

SERVING

Toasted flour tortillas

OPTIONAL TOPPINGS

Shredded cheese, avocado, salsa, hot sauce, cilantro

Place a 12-inch (30-cm) nonstick skillet over medium heat and add the sausage. Cook for 4 to 5 minutes, breaking it up with a spoon, until it's browned and cooked through. Transfer the cooked sausage to a plate lined with paper towels to drain. Use additional paper towels to blot any excess grease from the sausage, then transfer it to your 4- to 6-quart (3.8- to 5.5-L) slow cooker. Add the chopped sweet potato, Yukon Gold potato and Flavor Fiesta Taco Seasoning Mix, and toss the mixture to combine. Place the salsa, onion and chiles over the top.

Cover and cook on low until the potatoes are just barely fork-tender, 3 to 4 hours. Stir in the beans, cover and cook for an additional 30 to 60 minutes.

Add 2 tablespoons (28 g) of butter to a 12-inch (30-cm) nonstick skillet and place it over medium heat. When the butter has melted, crack 2 or 3 eggs into the skillet, cover and reduce the heat to low. Cook for 3 to 4 minutes, until the yolks have cooked to the desired level of doneness. Sprinkle with salt and pepper. Repeat with the remaining eggs.

For over-easy eggs, use a spatula to carefully flip the eggs halfway through the cooking time. Continue to cook to the desired level of doneness. For nicely shaped eggs, crack them, one at a time, into a small cup or ramekin, then gently pour them into the skillet.

Spoon the sausage, potato and bean mixture into serving bowls, top with the cooked eggs and serve with the toasted flour tortillas. Add the optional toppings, if desired.

OVERNIGHT SKILLET MAPLE-PECAN CINNAMON ROLLS

This make-ahead recipe allows you to stay in bed a little bit later in the morning and still include made-from-scratch cinnamon rolls on your breakfast or brunch menu. A batch of my dinner roll dough is rolled out and filled with a buttery, sweet, cinnamon-pecan filling. Let the rolls rest overnight in the refrigerator while you sleep, and in the morning, it's just a matter of popping them in the oven and whisking up the simple maple icing. Served warm, these are truly a heavenly treat.

YIELDS 10 ROLLS

1 batch of Perfectly Tender Skillet Dinner Roll dough (page 117)

1 tbsp (14 g) butter, softened

¼ cup (55 g) butter, melted

FILLING

¼ cup (40 g) brown sugar

¼ cup (50 g) granulated sugar

2 tsp (6 g) cinnamon

⅓ cup (40 g) chopped pecans

MAPLE ICING

1 cup (130 g) confectioners' sugar

2 tbsp (28 g) butter, melted

2 tbsp (30 ml) pure maple syrup

1 tbsp (15 ml) milk, or as needed

After preparing the dough, set it on a lightly floured board and let it rest for about 10 minutes.

Meanwhile, grease a 10-inch (25-cm) cast-iron or other heavy, ovenproof skillet with the softened butter.

Use a rolling pin to roll the dough out into a 12 × 14-inch (30 × 35-cm) rectangle. Pour the melted butter over the surface of the dough, and use a pastry brush to coat the entire surface evenly.

In a small bowl, combine the brown sugar, granulated sugar and cinnamon. Sprinkle the mixture evenly over the dough, then sprinkle it evenly with the pecans. Roll up the dough, from the shorter, 12-inch (30-cm) side into a log, forming and shaping the dough with your hands to make it as even as possible. Trim off the uneven ends of the roll, then slice the log into 10 equal-size rolls. Place the rolls in the skillet.

If you'd like to bake the rolls right away, cover the skillet with a clean kitchen towel and place it in a warm, draft-free place for 30 to 45 minutes. Alternatively, cover the dish with foil and refrigerate overnight or for at least 8 hours. Then, remove the foil and let it stand at room temperature for 30 minutes to take the chill off.

Preheat your oven to 350°F (175°C).

Bake the rolls for 20 to 25 minutes, until lightly golden brown. While the rolls are baking, whisk together in a small mixing bowl the confectioners' sugar, melted butter and maple syrup, adding as much milk as needed to reach a spreadable consistency.

Remove the rolls from the oven, and allow them to cool slightly for about 10 minutes. Spread them with the maple icing while they are still warm.

LEFTOVER HAM, SPINACH AND ROASTED RED PEPPER STRATA

This recipe is a great way to make use of leftover holiday ham. If you don't have leftover ham, you can still put this tasty strata together with a ham steak from the meat section of your grocery store. Assembling the strata and refrigerating it overnight allows you to get this dish cooking first thing in the morning for a late-morning brunch.

SERVES 10

1 lb (450 g) loaf of French bread

1 (10-oz [280-g]) package chopped frozen spinach, thawed

2 tbsp (28 g) butter

1 cup (150 g) diced onion

1 lb (450 g) leftover ham, cut into bite-size pieces (about 2 cups), divided

1 cup (110 g) chopped jarred roasted red peppers, divided

1½ cups (180 g) grated Havarti cheese, divided

1 cup (120 g) grated sharp cheddar cheese, divided

9 large eggs

2 cups (480 ml) milk

1 tbsp (15 g) Dijon mustard

½ tsp salt

¼ tsp pepper

NOTE: Each time you remove the cover during the cooking process, wipe down the condensation on its interior with a kitchen towel before you replace it.

Preheat the oven to 350°F (175°C). Generously coat the bottom and sides of the insert of your 6-quart (5.5-L) slow cooker with nonstick cooking spray.

Cut off and discard the ends of the loaf of French bread or save them for another use. Cut the bread into approximately 1-inch (3-cm) slices, then cut the slices into cubes. Scatter the bread on a rimmed baking sheet, and bake in the oven until lightly toasted, 5 to 7 minutes.

Meanwhile, enclose the thawed spinach between a double layer of paper towels, and use your hands to twist and squeeze it over the sink to drain as much liquid as possible. Set it aside.

Place a skillet over medium heat and add the butter. When the butter has melted, add the onions and sauté for 3 to 4 minutes, until softened.

Spread half of the toasted bread over the bottom of the slow cooker. Cover it with half of the well-drained spinach, onions, ham, roasted red peppers, and Havarti and cheddar cheeses. Press down on the top with your hands to compact the ingredients, then make another layer with the same remaining ingredients.

Whisk the eggs with the milk, Dijon mustard, salt and pepper in a large mixing bowl. Pour the egg mixture evenly over the top of the strata, cover and cook on low for 3 to 4 hours, until the center appears set. To test for doneness, insert a butter knife into the center. The egg custard should be cooked and not runny.

Turn off the slow cooker, and allow the strata to rest for 10 minutes before slicing and serving.

MAKE-AHEAD METHOD
Assemble the strata as directed in a removable slow-cooker insert. Cover and transfer the insert to your refrigerator to chill overnight. Keep in mind that if the slow-cooker insert is chilled, it will slow down the cooking process, possibly resulting in a longer cook time, so plan accordingly.

MAPLE-PEANUT BUTTER GRANOLA

This nutty granola is lightly sweetened with pure maple syrup and honey. You can customize it with your favorite dried fruits and sprinkle it over Greek yogurt with a drizzle of honey for a quick breakfast or afternoon snack. Sprinkle in some chocolate chips after it has cooled and you've got yourself an irresistible snacking granola with a heavenly peanut butter–chocolate flavor combination.

YIELDS APPROXIMATELY 3½ QUARTS (1.7 KG)

4 cups (360 g) old-fashioned oats

1 cup (120 g) chopped unsalted or lightly salted peanuts

1 cup (120 g) chopped unsalted almonds

½ cup (130 g) unsalted sunflower kernels

1 cup (75 g) unsweetened coconut flakes (not shredded)

½ tsp salt

½ cup (90 g) creamy peanut butter

¼ cup (60 g) coconut oil

¼ cup (40 g) brown sugar

¼ cup (60 ml) pure maple syrup

¼ cup (60 ml) honey

1 cup (145 g) dried fruit such as raisins, cranberries or cherries, optional

1 cup (175 g) chocolate chips, optional

Generously coat a 6-quart (5.5-L) slow cooker with nonstick cooking spray.

Combine the oats, peanuts, almonds, sunflower kernels, coconut flakes and salt in the slow cooker, and toss with a spoon until the mixture is well combined.

Place the peanut butter, coconut oil and brown sugar in a small microwave-safe bowl, and microwave on high for 30 seconds, until the peanut butter and coconut oil have melted. Stir in the maple syrup and honey, and pour the wet mixture over the oat mixture in the slow cooker. Stir until all of the dry ingredients are well coated.

Cover the slow cooker, leaving the cover slightly offset so that there is about a 1-inch (2.5-cm) air gap to allow for airflow during the cooking process, and cook for 2½ hours on high. Stir the granola every 20 to 30 minutes by pushing a spoon all the way down to the bottom of the slow cooker and up. If some of the pieces start to burn, set the slow cooker to low, and continue to cook until the mixture appears golden brown throughout. Don't worry if it appears a bit soft, it will crisp up as it cools.

Spread the cooked granola out on to a large sheet of foil to cool completely. Once completely cooled, add dried fruit, chocolate chips or 1 cup (160 g) total of both if you like!

> **TIP** If you are using shredded coconut instead of the large flaked variety, it should be added at the end with the optional add-ins, as it will likely burn if added at the beginning of the cooking time.

ROAST BEEF HASH AND EGGS

This easy skillet breakfast is a great way to use up leftover roast beef or, honestly, any type of leftover meat you might have on hand. No leftovers? Just ask for a ½" (1-cm)-thick slice of roast beef at the deli counter to make it any time the craving strikes.

I recommend using the refrigerated diced hash brown potatoes available in most supermarkets. They are such a great time saver! If you are using frozen potatoes, be sure they are completely thawed before beginning.

SERVES 4

2 tbsp (28 g) butter

1 tbsp (15 ml) vegetable oil

1 (20-oz [560-g]) package refrigerated diced potatoes (I like Simply Potatoes)

½ cup (75 g) diced sweet yellow onion

½ cup (55 g) diced green or red bell pepper

1 tbsp (3 g) fresh thyme leaves

1 tsp paprika

½ tsp salt, plus more to taste

¼ tsp freshly ground black pepper, plus more to taste

¼ tsp granulated garlic

½ lb (225 g) cooked roast beef or deli roast beef, sliced ½" (1-cm) thick, cut into ½" (1-cm) pieces

4–6 large eggs

2 tbsp (6 g) chopped fresh parsley

Preheat the oven to 400°F (200°C).

Melt the butter with the vegetable oil in a 12-inch (30-cm) cast-iron skillet over medium-high heat. Add the potatoes, onion and bell pepper, and cook for about 4 to 5 minutes, stirring occasionally, until the onion and bell pepper have softened and the potatoes are lightly browned. Season with the thyme, paprika, salt, pepper and granulated garlic. Stir again, scraping up any browned bits from the bottom of the skillet.

Reduce the heat to medium, and use a wooden spoon or spatula to flatten the mixture down into an even layer. Cook undisturbed until it is crisp and browned on the bottom, about 3 to 4 minutes. Add the roast beef, stir the mixture to combine it well, then flatten it down once more and cook undisturbed for another 2 to 3 minutes.

Using a spoon, make four to six indentations in the hash and crack an egg into each. Transfer the skillet to the oven, and bake until the egg whites are set and the yolks are cooked as desired, 9 to 11 minutes. Season with additional salt and pepper, and sprinkle with parsley before serving.

> **TIP:** Thyme leaves are usually small enough that you won't need to chop them. Instead, hold a sprig of thyme by the top so that the leaves are pointing upward, and slide your fingers down the woody stalk to strip off the leaves.

SWEETS

You might be surprised to find a chapter devoted to sweets in a slow-cooker cookbook, especially since quick breads are among the recipes! While unconventional, the slow cooker is a wonderful option for preparing desserts when you need to free up oven space or don't want to heat up the kitchen. This chapter is full of simple and comforting desserts, like Apple Crisp (page 176), Gingerbread Bread Pudding with Spiced-Rum Cream Sauce (page 167) and Skillet Blackberry-Almond Peach Cobbler (page 172).

When preparing quick breads and other "baked" items in your slow cooker, it's important to use the high setting so that they rise properly. Your unit may also have hot spots that can cause uneven cooking. If this is the case, lift the slow-cooker insert about halfway through the cooking time and rotate it to help distribute the heat more evenly.

To avoid any issues with condensation, you can set a double layer of paper towels over the top of the slow-cooker insert and then set the cover on top. Or lift the cover carefully to prevent the moisture from dripping into the slow cooker, and use a clean kitchen towel to thoroughly dry the inside of the cover before replacing it.

GINGERBREAD BREAD PUDDING WITH SPICED-RUM CREAM SAUCE

This may be one of the most comforting desserts in existence. When I cook bread pudding in a conventional oven, I always set it in a water bath, but the moist environment of the slow cooker eliminates this step, and the result is perfection. You can line your slow cooker with a foil collar (see the Tip below), but personally, I love those crispy edges!

SERVES 8

GINGERBREAD BREAD PUDDING

1 (1-lb [450-g]) loaf French bread

5 large eggs

1½ cups (360 ml) heavy whipping cream

1½ cups (360 ml) milk

¾ cup (165 g) dark brown sugar

¼ cup (60 ml) unsulphured molasses

2 tsp (10 ml) pure vanilla extract

2 tsp (6 g) ground cinnamon

1 tsp ginger

¼ tsp ground allspice

¼ tsp ground cloves

¼ tsp salt

½ cup (76 g) golden raisins

SPICED-RUM CREAM SAUCE

6 tbsp (60 g) sugar

2 tbsp (20 g) cornstarch

2 cups (480 ml) heavy whipping cream or half-and-half

2 tbsp (30 ml) spiced rum (I like Captain Morgan®) or 2 tsp (10 ml) rum extract or pure vanilla extract

½ tsp ground nutmeg, plus more for serving, optional

Preheat the oven to 350°F (175°C). Generously coat the insert of a 6-quart (5.5-L) slow cooker with nonstick cooking spray.

Cut off and discard the ends of the bread (or save them for another use). Cut it into 1-inch (3-cm) slices, then tear each slice into ½-inch (1-cm) pieces. Scatter the pieces of bread on a rimmed baking sheet, and bake for 5 to 7 minutes, until lightly toasted.

In a large mixing bowl, whisk together the eggs, cream, milk, brown sugar, molasses, vanilla extract, cinnamon, ginger, allspice, cloves and salt. Set it aside.

Transfer the toasted bread cubes to the slow cooker, and sprinkle them with the raisins. Pour the egg mixture over the top, and stir, from the bottom up, until all of the bread is well coated. Use a spatula or the back of a spoon to press the mixture down into an even layer. Cover and cook for 3 hours on low, until a knife inserted in the center comes out clean.

As soon as the bread pudding is ready, whisk together the sugar and cornstarch in a heavy saucepan. Slowly whisk in the cream, and place the pan over medium heat. Cook for about 3 or 4 minutes, stirring, until the sugar is dissolved and the mixture is slightly thickened. Remove the pan from the heat, and stir in the spiced rum and the nutmeg. The sauce will continue to thicken a bit as it sits.

Serve the warm bread pudding in individual serving bowls with a drizzle of the warm sauce and a sprinkling of nutmeg, if desired.

> TIP: Many slow cookers generate more heat on one side, which can result in burned edges. Try lining your slow-cooker insert with a foil collar. Fold two 18-inch (45-cm) pieces of foil into 4-inch (10-cm) strips, and place them along the edges of the insert. Spray them with nonstick cooking spray, and proceed with the recipe.

CHOCOLATE-BUTTERSCOTCH MIXED-NUT CANDY CLUSTERS

Chocolate nut clusters are a Christmas tradition in many homes, but I am a firm believer that these tasty candies should not be reserved for just the holiday season. Since my boys have always loved the chocolate-butterscotch flavor combo, my version of this classic candy includes both chocolate and butterscotch baking chips along with peanuts and some coarsely chopped almonds for even more interest.

You can dress them with festive holiday sprinkles for Valentine's Day, the Fourth of July, Halloween or Christmas, and they are just as tasty in their pure, unadorned form any time of year.

YIELDS APPROXIMATELY 70 TO 80 CANDIES

2 lb (910 g) almond bark, broken into pieces

1 (12-oz [340-g]) package semisweet chocolate chips

1 (12-oz [340-g]) package dark (bittersweet) chocolate chips

1 (12-oz [340-g]) package butterscotch baking chips

3 cups (360 g) roasted, salted peanuts

2 cups (240 g) roughly chopped roasted, salted almonds

70–80 mini baking cups

Assorted sprinkles, for decorating, optional

Layer the almond bark, semisweet, bittersweet and butterscotch baking chips, peanuts and almonds in that order in the insert of a 6-quart (5.5-L) slow cooker. Don't stir. Cover and set the slow cooker to low for 2 hours. After the first hour, remove the cover and stir the mixture. It won't be completely melted at this point. Cover and continue to cook for the remaining 1 hour, until the mixture is completely melted and smooth when stirred. You may not need to cook it for the entire 2 hours. Once the mixture is completely melted, stir it well and set the slow cooker to the warm setting while you work.

Arrange the mini baking cups on two baking sheets. Use a small cookie scoop to divide the mixture between the cups. Decorate the cups with sprinkles before the chocolate sets, if desired. Allow the candies to cool completely at room temperature until set. If you'd like to set them more quickly, transfer the baking sheets to the refrigerator and chill the candies for about 1 hour.

Store the candies in an airtight container separated by layers of wax paper for up to 3 days, or refrigerate them for up to 2 weeks. To keep them fresh longer, freeze them solid on a baking sheet and then transfer them to plastic freezer bags, pressing out as much air as possible before sealing and placing them in the freezer. Frozen candies will keep well for up to 2 months.

> **TIP:** The cleanest, easiest way to transfer the candy mixture to the baking cups is to use a small cookie scoop. It works like a dream.

GIANT PRETZEL DOUBLE CHOCOLATE CHIP COOKIE

This giant cookie is a great example of the large variety of tasks your slow cooker can pull off. Testing this recipe felt somewhat like conducting a science experiment: Would it work? Why, yes, it does!

The massive cookie is loaded with both bittersweet and semisweet chocolate chips, as well as salted pretzel sticks for a delicious sweet-and-salty flavor combination. Add a scoop of ice cream and a drizzle of hot fudge to impress your cookie fans. It's a completely unexpected but really fun baking project.

SERVES 6 TO 8

1½ cups (190 g) all-purpose flour

1 tsp baking soda

½ tsp salt

½ cup (115 g) butter, softened

½ cup (95 g) granulated sugar

½ cup (110 g) packed light brown sugar

1 large egg

2 tsp (10 ml) pure vanilla extract

¾ cup (130 g) dark (bittersweet) chocolate chips

½ cup (90 g) semisweet chocolate chips

½ cup (35 g) broken-up salted pretzel sticks

TIP: Break the pretzels sticks into small pieces using your hands. If you use a mallet or rolling pin, you will pulverize the pretzels, and we want pieces, not pretzel dust.

Cut off two sheets of foil about 14 inches (35 cm) long, the width of a 6-quart (5.5-L) slow cooker. Fold the foil sheets in half and then in half again. Place one of the sheets along the bottom of the slow-cooker insert lengthwise, and place the other crosswise over the top to create a foil sling. Spray the foil and the slow-cooker insert generously with nonstick cooking spray.

Combine the flour, baking soda and salt in a medium mixing bowl and set it aside.

Place the softened butter in a large mixing bowl, add the granulated sugar and brown sugar, and beat with an electric mixer until the mixture is creamy. Add the egg and vanilla extract, and beat again to combine. Add the flour mixture to the butter mixture, and mix again until it reaches a nice dough-like consistency. Use a spoon to fold in the bittersweet and semisweet chocolate chips and pretzel pieces.

Spoon the dough into the slow cooker on top of the foil sling, and press it down into an even layer with your hands. Place a double layer of paper towels over the top of the slow cooker's rim, and place the cover on top.

Cook for 2 hours on high. After the first hour of the cooking time, use oven mitts to carefully lift and rotate the insert to ensure the cookie will bake evenly. Continue to cook for the remaining 1 hour, or just until the cookie is set in the center and golden brown around the edges. It may take less than 1 hour, so watch it closely. Turn off and unplug the slow cooker, and using oven mitts, carefully remove the ceramic insert from the slow cooker. Let the cookie rest in the slow-cooker insert for 30 minutes, then use the tops of the foil sling to lift the cookie out of the insert and onto a rack or cutting board to cool completely before serving.

SKILLET BLACKBERRY-ALMOND PEACH COBBLER

This spectacular summer dessert uses fresh peaches and blackberries at their peak. A soft cobbler dough and buttered, sweetened sliced almonds are scattered over the top, and the whole thing is baked in a 12-inch (30-cm) skillet until bubbly and browned. Serve it with a scoop of vanilla ice cream or a dollop of freshly whipped cream.

SERVES 6

FILLING

2 lbs (910 g) fresh peaches, peeled and sliced (about 3 or 4 large peaches)

6 oz (170 g) fresh blackberries, rinsed and drained

¼ tsp almond extract

¼ tsp pure vanilla extract

½ cup (95 g) sugar

3 tbsp (30 g) cornstarch

2 tbsp (28 g) butter

COBBLER DOUGH

1 cup (125 g) flour

½ cup (95 g) sugar

1 tsp baking powder

Pinch of salt

6 tbsp (90 g) butter, melted

¼ cup (60 ml) heavy cream

2 tbsp (28 g) butter, for the skillet

ALMOND TOPPING

½ cup (60 g) sliced almonds

2 tbsp (25) sugar

2 tbsp (28 g) butter, melted

Preheat the oven to 375°F (190°C).

Add the peaches and blackberries to a large mixing bowl, and toss them with the almond and vanilla extracts. Add the sugar and cornstarch. Toss to combine them with the fruit and set aside.

To make the cobbler dough, combine the flour, sugar, baking powder and salt in a medium mixing bowl. Add the melted butter and cream, and stir to form a soft dough. Set it aside.

Add the solid butter to a 12-inch (30-cm) cast-iron skillet and place it over medium heat. When the butter has melted, remove the skillet from the heat and swirl the butter around the skillet to coat it evenly. Add the peach and berry mixture to the skillet, along with all the juices that have accumulated in the bowl. Scatter bits of the cobbler dough over the top. There will be gaps, and there's no need to fuss too much to make it neat. This is a rustic dessert!

For the topping, combine the almonds, sugar and melted butter in a small bowl, and scatter the mixture over the top of the cobbler dough.

Transfer the skillet to the preheated oven and bake for 25 to 30 minutes, until bubbly and golden brown. If you notice the top getting too dark, set a sheet of foil lightly on top of the skillet for the remainder of the baking time.

Now comes the hard part: let the cobbler cool for 15 to 20 minutes before serving. The juices will thicken and set up, and it will be wonderfully warm and ready for serving.

> **TIP:** To easily peel peaches, bring a pot of water to boil and use a sharp knife to slice a large X across the bottom of each peach. Boil them for 30 seconds, then transfer them to a bowl of ice water. When cool enough to handle, the skins will pull off easily.

GLAZED LEMON-BLUEBERRY BREAD

I'm sure the last thing you had in mind when you purchased your slow cooker was using it to bake breads and cakes. Well, you are not alone; I too was very surprised to discover how well it works! The moist, velvety texture in this bread is amazing. I've found that a loaf pan yields the best result when baking quick breads in a slow cooker. It eliminates many issues, especially for lighter-colored and more tender cakes and breads, which tend to get too dark on the edges baked directly in the slow cooker insert.

SERVES 8

1½ cups (190 g) all-purpose flour

1 tsp baking powder

¼ tsp baking soda

¼ tsp salt

1 cup (190 g) sugar

2 large eggs

⅓ cup (80 ml) vegetable oil

1 lemon, zested and halved, divided

½ tsp pure vanilla extract

½ cup (120 g) sour cream

1 cup (100 g) blueberries, rinsed and drained well

½ cup (65 g) powdered sugar

TIP: To ensure even baking, use oven mitts to lift and turn the slow-cooker insert (with the lid in place) about halfway through the cooking time.

Coat an 8 × 4-inch (20 × 10-cm) loaf pan with nonstick cooking spray. If the loaf pan is too large to sit level on the bottom of your 6- to 7-quart (5.5- to 6.6-L) slow-cooker insert, cut off a sheet of foil about 24 inches (60 cm) long and roll it up into a cylinder. Shape the cylinder into an oval to create a foil rack, and place it in the bottom of your slow cooker.

Add the flour, baking powder, baking soda and salt to a medium mixing bowl, and whisk the mixture until combined. Set it aside.

In a large mixing bowl, use an electric mixer to combine the sugar and eggs. Add the vegetable oil, lemon zest, juice from half of the lemon and the vanilla. Mix again until well combined. Add the dry mixture to the wet mixture all at once, and use a spoon to mix it until just combined. Stir in the sour cream. Fold in the blueberries, and mix lightly until the berries are incorporated throughout the batter.

Spoon the batter into the loaf pan, and place it in the slow cooker, balanced on top of the foil rack, if using, making sure the pan is level.

Cover and cook for 2½ to 3 hours on high, until the bread is golden brown at the edges and a toothpick or cake tester inserted in the center of the bread comes out clean.

Turn the slow cooker off, and with oven mitts, carefully remove the loaf pan from the slow-cooker insert. Let the bread cool in the pan for 15 to 20 minutes, then turn the bread out onto a piece of parchment or wax paper and allow it to cool completely.

Combine the powdered sugar with just enough lemon juice from the remaining half of the lemon to make a glaze that is thin enough to drizzle over the completely cooled bread.

This bread can also be baked in a conventional oven at 350°F (175°C) for 45 to 55 minutes.

APPLE CRISP

This Apple Crisp is at the top of my list of slow-cooker dessert favorites. Apples cook to tender perfection, releasing their juices to combine with a cinnamon- and nutmeg-spiced brown sugar mixture. I like to use crisp-sweet apples, like Gala or Envy, and throw in a couple of tart-sweet Granny Smiths for good measure.

The apple crisp will be piping hot at the end of the cooking time and will need to cool to a suitable temperature for serving. By allowing it to rest with the cover offset, you'll have to wait for only 20 to 30 minutes before serving. The additional air circulation also helps the oat crumble to crisp up as it cools.

SERVES 6

CRUMBLE TOPPING

1 cup (90 g) old-fashioned oats (not quick-cooking oats)

¾ cup (95 g) all-purpose flour

½ cup (75 g) brown sugar

1 tsp cinnamon

¼ tsp nutmeg

Pinch of salt

½ cup (115 g) butter, softened

APPLE FILLING

3½ lbs (1.6 kg) assorted crisp-sweet and tart-sweet apples (like Gala, Envy and Granny Smith), peeled, cored and sliced ¼" (5-mm) thick

⅓ cup (75 g) brown sugar

¼ cup (50 g) granulated sugar

1 tbsp (10 g) cornstarch

1½ tsp (5 g) ground cinnamon

¼ tsp ground ginger

¼ tsp ground nutmeg

Vanilla ice cream, for serving

For the topping, place the oats, flour, brown sugar, cinnamon, nutmeg, salt and butter in a medium mixing bowl. Use a fork or pastry blender to combine well, then knead the mixture with your fingers until it's crumbly. Set aside.

Coat the insert of a 6-quart (5.5-L) slow cooker with nonstick cooking spray. Place the apple slices inside the slow cooker.

To make the filling, in a small mixing bowl whisk together the brown sugar, granulated sugar, cornstarch, cinnamon, ginger and nutmeg. Sprinkle the sugar mixture over the apples in the slow cooker, and toss to combine. Sprinkle the crumbled oat mixture evenly over the top. Place a double layer of paper towels over the top of the slow-cooker insert to catch any condensation or use a kitchen towel to periodically wipe the lid dry while cooking, and place the cover on top. Cook for 3 to 4 hours on low or for 2 hours on high, until the apples are fork-tender.

Power off and unplug the slow cooker. Remove the cover and paper towels, if using. Wipe the inside of the cover down with a clean kitchen towel to dry any condensation, then replace the cover crosswise over the slow cooker, leaving the edges open to the air. Let it sit for 20 to 30 minutes to cool and for the filling to continue to set up.

Spoon the crisp into serving bowls with a scoop or two of vanilla ice cream.

BUTTERMILK BANANA BREAD

I often buy buttermilk for use in other recipes and have just a bit leftover—and then there are those brown-spotted, overripe bananas staring at me from the fruit bowl. Along with pantry staples, this recipe uses these two items to create a pleasing, traditional quick bread. It will bake up beautifully in either your slow cooker or conventional oven.

SERVES 8

1¾ cups (220 g) all-purpose flour

1 tsp baking soda

½ tsp salt

1 cup (190 g) sugar

½ cup (115 g) butter, softened

2 medium ripe bananas

2 large eggs

⅓ cup (80 ml) buttermilk

2 tsp (10 ml) pure vanilla extract

¾ cup (90 g) chopped walnuts

Powdered sugar, optional

Coat an 8 × 4-inch (20 × 10-cm) loaf pan with nonstick cooking spray. If the loaf pan is too large to sit level on the bottom of your 6 to 7-quart (5.5- to 6.6-L) slow-cooker insert, cut off a sheet of foil about 24 inches (60 cm) long and roll it up into a cylinder. Shape the cylinder into an oval to create a foil rack, and place it in the bottom of your slow cooker.

In a small bowl, stir together the flour, baking soda and salt, and set it aside.

In a large bowl, use an electric hand mixer to combine the sugar, butter, bananas, eggs, buttermilk and vanilla. Pour the flour mixture into the wet mixture, and use a spoon to stir it until just combined. Fold in the walnuts.

Spoon the batter into the loaf pan, and place it in the slow cooker, balanced on top of the foil rack, if using, making sure the pan is level. Place a double layer of paper towels over the top of the slow-cooker insert to catch any condensation or use a kitchen towel to periodically wipe the lid dry while cooking.

Cover and cook for 2 to 2½ hours on high, until a skewer comes out mostly clean. If you're not using the paper towel layer, carefully lift the cover so condensation won't drip onto the surface of the bread. Wipe down the inside of the cover with a kitchen towel before replacing it.

Turn the slow cooker off, and with oven mitts, carefully remove the loaf pan from the slow-cooker insert. Let the bread cool in the pan for 15 to 20 minutes, then turn the bread out onto a piece of parchment or wax paper and allow it to cool completely.

Sprinkle the completely cooled bread with powdered sugar, if desired.

This bread can also be baked in a conventional oven at 350°F (175°C) for 45 to 55 minutes.

CINNAMON-APPLE YOGURT BREAD

This is absolutely delicious on its own or dusted with powdered sugar, but it is outstanding with luscious cream cheese–walnut frosting. A slice is just the thing with a hot cup of tea in the afternoon or served with scrambled eggs for a sweet addition to breakfast.

SERVES 8

CINNAMON-APPLE YOGURT BREAD

1¼ cups (155 g) all-purpose flour

1 tsp baking soda

½ tsp baking powder

1½ tsp (5 g) cinnamon

½ tsp ground nutmeg

¼ tsp cloves

¼ tsp salt

1 cup (190 g) granulated sugar

½ cup (115 g) butter, softened

2 large eggs

1 tsp pure vanilla extract

¾ cup (180 g) Greek yogurt, divided

1 cup (100 g) peeled, diced apple

⅓ cup (40 g) chopped walnuts

CREAM CHEESE-WALNUT FROSTING

3 oz (85 g) cream cheese, softened

2 tbsp (28 g) butter, softened

¾ cup (100 g) powdered sugar

½ tsp pure vanilla extract

½ tsp fresh lemon juice

¼ cup (30 g) chopped walnuts, for topping

Coat an 8 × 4-inch (20 × 10-cm) loaf pan with nonstick cooking spray. If the loaf pan is too large to sit level on the bottom of your 6- to 7-quart (5.5- to 6.6-L) slow-cooker insert, cut off a sheet of foil about 24 inches (60 cm) long and roll it up into a cylinder. Shape the cylinder into an oval to create a foil rack, and place it in the bottom of your slow cooker.

In a medium mixing bowl, combine the flour, baking soda, baking powder, cinnamon, nutmeg, cloves and salt. Set it aside.

In a large mixing bowl, combine the sugar and butter, mixing for several minutes. Add the eggs and vanilla extract, and continue mixing until well combined.

Add half of the flour mixture to the wet mixture, and stir it with a wooden spoon until just barely incorporated. Add half of the Greek yogurt, and stir again until the mixture is moistened. Repeat with the remaining flour mixture and yogurt, taking care not to overmix. Fold the diced apple and walnuts into the batter.

Spoon the batter into the loaf pan and place it in the slow cooker, balanced on top of the foil rack, if using, making sure the pan is level.

Cover and cook for 2½ to 3 hours on high, until a toothpick or cake tester inserted in center of the loaf comes out clean.

Turn the slow cooker off, and with oven mitts, carefully remove the loaf pan from the slow-cooker insert. Let the bread cool in the pan for 15 to 20 minutes, then turn the bread out onto a piece of parchment or wax paper and allow it to cool completely before frosting.

Use an electric mixer to beat the cream cheese together with the softened butter in a medium bowl. Add the powdered sugar, and mix again until well incorporated. Add the vanilla and lemon juice, and beat until creamy.

Frost the cooled bread, and immediately sprinkle it with the chopped walnuts.

This bread can also be baked in a conventional oven at 350°F (175°C) for 45 to 55 minutes.

SPICE MIXES

These homemade seasoning blends are used in many of the recipes in this cookbook, and they're also staples in my kitchen. While I'm a fan of some store-bought mixes, especially Italian seasoning and blends like garam masala, I've found that the seasoning mixes in this chapter are so much better when made at home.

The Kickin' Cajun Seasoning Mix (page 184) is an easy way to add a ton of flavor to recipes like my Cajun Barbecue Ribs (page 53) and Jambalaya Pasta (page 86). And unlike with store-bought Cajun seasoning, it is super easy to control the level of heat by adjusting the amounts of either the red pepper flakes or cayenne pepper.

Best-Ever Barbecue Seasoning Mix (page 185) adds rich, smoky flavor to a variety of dishes, including easy, one-pot Barbecue Turkey Joes (page 38), Honey Barbecue Snack Mix (page 138) and slow-cooker Barbecue Chicken Drumsticks (page 34).

I always have a batch of each of these seasoning mixes in my pantry and try to incorporate them in my recipes whenever possible. It is such a wonderful timesaver to reach for just one jar instead of hunting down a list of spices when I'm rushed to get dinner on the table.

KICKIN' CAJUN SEASONING MIX

This Cajun blend of spices is the highest-rated seasoning mix on Valerie's Kitchen. It is a fantastic dry rub for pan-seared seafood or grilled meats. As the name implies, it delivers a spicy kick, as any good Cajun spice mix should. It is easy to create a milder mix by reducing the amount of cayenne pepper.

YIELDS ABOUT 5 TBSP (45 G)

1 tbsp (9 g) onion powder

2 tsp (6 g) garlic powder

2 tsp (6 g) smoked paprika

2 tsp (2 g) dried thyme

2 tsp (2 g) dried oregano

2 tsp (6 g) finely ground sea salt

1 tsp freshly ground black pepper

1 tsp cayenne pepper, or to taste

Add the onion powder, garlic powder, paprika, thyme, oregano, salt, black pepper and cayenne pepper to a small mason jar or airtight container. Seal it with the lid and shake well to combine. Store the seasoning mix on a cool, dry pantry shelf.

FLAVOR FIESTA TACO SEASONING MIX

Since Mexican food is on our menu every week, this is the seasoning mix I use most frequently. It adds great flavor to a variety of Mexican dishes in a far more pleasing way than the packets you find at the grocery store. As written, it will add very little heat to your recipes, but you can adjust the amount of red pepper flakes as needed to suit your taste.

YIELDS ABOUT 9 TBSP (81 G)

¼ cup (36 g) chili powder

2 tbsp (18 g) ground cumin

2 tsp (6 g) paprika

2 tsp (6 g) finely ground sea salt

2 tsp (6 g) freshly ground black pepper

1 tsp granulated garlic or garlic powder

1 tsp onion powder

1 tsp dried oregano

½ tsp red pepper flakes, or to taste

Add the chili powder, cumin, paprika, salt, pepper, granulated garlic, onion powder, oregano and red pepper flakes to a small mason jar or airtight container. Seal it with the lid and shake well to combine. Store the seasoning mix on a cool, dry pantry shelf.

BEST-EVER BARBECUE SEASONING MIX

I love this smoky, slightly sweet mix for adding classic barbecue flavor to everything from grilled meats to roasted potatoes. This is a flavorful component to several of the recipes in this book.

YIELDS ABOUT 5 TBSP (45 G)

2 tbsp (18 g) smoked paprika

1 tbsp (9 g) chili powder

1 tbsp (9 g) brown sugar

1½ tsp (4 g) finely ground sea salt

1 tsp granulated garlic or garlic powder

1 tsp onion powder

½ tsp freshly ground black pepper, or to taste

¼ tsp cayenne pepper, or to taste

Add the paprika, chili powder, brown sugar, salt, granulated garlic, onion powder, black pepper and cayenne pepper to a small mason jar or airtight container. Seal it with the lid and shake well to combine. Store the seasoning mix on a cool, dry pantry shelf.

SMOKY FAJITA SEASONING MIX

Use this Smoky Fajita Seasoning Mix as a dry rub or mix it with equal parts olive oil to create a wet rub that will deliciously enhance shrimp, chicken, pork or beef. Use 1 to 2 tablespoons (9 to 18 g) of seasoning mix per pound (450 g) of meat.

YIELDS ABOUT 8 TBSP (72 G)

2 tbsp (18 g) chili powder

2 tbsp (18 g) cumin

1 tbsp (9 g) smoked paprika

1 tbsp (9 g) finely ground sea salt

2 tsp (6 g) brown sugar

1 tsp freshly ground black pepper

1 tsp onion powder

1 tsp granulated garlic or garlic powder

½ tsp cayenne pepper, or to taste

Add the chili powder, cumin, paprika, salt, brown sugar, black pepper, onion powder, granulated garlic and cayenne pepper to a small mason jar or airtight container. Seal it with the lid and shake well to combine. Store the seasoning mix on a cool, dry pantry shelf.

ACKNOWLEDGMENTS

I want to thank my mom, Margaret Bolin. I would not be doing what I'm doing now without her guidance and the example she set as a fierce cook and accomplished baker for our very lucky family of eight. She's no longer here with us in the physical sense, but she's ever-present in my kitchen, standing next to me and whispering her words of incredible kitchen wisdom. I feel her presence every time I roll out a pie crust or start up the now-vintage KitchenAid mixer she bought for me as a birthday gift over 30 years ago and which I will never part with, no matter how many newfangled appliances come my way. And, to Dad, thank you for being such a shining example of loyalty, dedication and discipline. I'm certain that all of my hard-working, never-give-up genes came from you. You are loved more than you will ever know.

A huge heartfelt thank you to my husband, Paul, for your unending patience and positive attitude while three slow cookers ran almost non-stop in our kitchen for over six months during the recipe testing phase of this book. Our "days off" included romantic trips to the grocery store and a never-ending pile of dishes in the sink that you happily washed as soon as you walked in the door from work. Thank you for surviving the incessant ramblings of recipe concepts on pretty much a daily basis and the glow from my iPad at three in the morning when an idea struck in the middle of the night. Cookbook writing has even further reinforced that choosing you was the best choice I've made in my life by a long shot.

To my oldest son, Ryan, who said to me one day about ten years ago, "Mom, you need a blog," and then kept saying it until I did it. Thanks, honey. You have always been wise beyond your years. I am eternally grateful for my boys Adam, Connor and Jake and for Jake's girlfriend, Mina—my sweet little guinea pigs, happily taste-testing each and every recipe and providing very helpful feedback. I love you all to the moon and back.

Special thanks go to my son Jake for handling all of my technical issues, assisting in photo shoots and for his mad editing skills. I couldn't do what I do without you, and I am proud beyond words of all of your abilities.

So much love goes to my sisters, Nancy, Linda, Barbara and Marj. I grew up in a house where everyone learned to love food and to love to cook, and as a result, all of my sisters are forces to be reckoned with in the kitchen. As the youngest, I was surrounded by this circle of cooks and it has had a huge and lasting effect on me. Nancy, you are dearly missed by your family and your love of cooking and zest for life has made an indelible mark on all of us, but especially on your kids, whom I know will carry it forward into the next generation.

To my brother, Jim. Being the lone boy in a pack of girls made you the man you are today. You taught me at a very young age that it is very cool for guys to cook, and you do it so incredibly well. You got the very best from both Mom and Dad, and I know that you've made them both so proud. Thanks to the sweetest, funniest, best lookin' brother in the world.

I have endless gratitude and a great big place in my heart for my blog readers. You've made Valerie's Kitchen what it is today and have made it possible for me to move forward in this crazy, exhausting, completely amazing career.

To the food blogging community, which has provided me with so much encouragement and support over the years. I'm proud to be part of this community of ridiculously hard-working and smart self-starters. Special thanks to Amy for what started as hours upon hours of blog business talk that has now evolved into a close and valued friendship.

And, finally, thank you to Page Street Publishing for reaching out and making my dream of being a published cookbook author a reality. You've made it a pleasure to tackle this new experience.

ABOUT THE AUTHOR

Valerie Brunmeier is the founder, author and photographer behind the food blog Valerie's Kitchen, where she shares practical, approachable recipes to help busy home cooks create simple but delicious meals. Her recipes have been featured in many online publications, including *Better Homes & Gardens*, *Good Housekeeping*, *Redbook*, *Country Living*, *Cosmopolitan*, *Buzzfeed*, MSN and *Shape Magazine*. Valerie is a native Californian and currently resides in San Jose, a short fifteen-minute drive from the house where she grew up, with her husband, Paul, and three of her four sons. You can connect with her at fromvalerieskitchen.com.

INDEX